LECTURES
on the FIRST
CORINTHIANS

Volume 1

LECTURES
on the FIRST
CORINTHIANS
Volume 1

Dr. Jaerock Lee

LECTURES ON THE FIRST CORINTHIANS:
Volume 1 by Dr. Jaerock Lee
Published by Urim Books (Representative: Kyungtae Noh)
73, Yeouidaebang-ro 22-gil, Dongjak-Gu, Seoul, Korea
www.urimbooks.com

Unless otherwise noted, all Scripture quotations are taken from the Holy Bible,
NEW AMERICAN STANDARD BIBLE, ®, Copyright © 1960, 1962, 1963,
1968, 1971, 1972, 1973, 1975, 1977, 1995 by The Lockman Foundation.
Used by permission.

Copyright © 2010 by Dr. Jaerock Lee
ISBN: 978-89-7557-305-7(03230), ISBN: 978-7557-304-0(04230)(set)
Translated by Dr. Esther K. Chung. Used by permission.

Previously published in Korean by Urim Books, Seoul, Korea.
Copyright © 2008 by Dr Jaerock Lee,
ISBN: 978-89-7557-155-8(03230), ISBN: 978-7557-154-1(04230)(set)

First Published March 2010

Edited by Dr. Geumsun Vin
Designed by Editorial Bureau of Urim Books
Printed by Yewon Printing Company
For more information contact at urimbook@hotmail.com

Spiritual and Physical Guidance for Believers

People who live in the modern world may wander around or have conflict within themselves because of the confusion of values. This is not restricted to only non-believers, but we may all face various problems even while we lead a life in faith. Those problems may include disagreements, differences in opinion, law-suits, marriage and divorce.

The enemy devil and Satan continually tempt believers to cause them to live outside the Word of God. Thus those who try to live by the Word of God may have questions about the Word and its practical application to solve problems.

So was the case with the church in Corinth. Corinth at the time of Paul was a busy city with many people from various cultures and diverse ethnic backgrounds. There were definitive social classes and the population worshipped a number of different gods. There was also a great deal of moral corruption.

Living under such conditions, the believers in the church of Corinth had many conflicts and problems. Furthermore, since the church was newly established, they had difficulties in leading a life in faith. To help them lead a mature Christian life, the apostle Paul gave them biblical answers to many such questions and problems.

These answers and a way to solve many of these problems that can take place in our everyday lives are recorded in Paul's first letter to the church of Corinth known as 1 Corinthians. In today's complex society it is important that we carefully learn and understand its content.

This book, *Lectures on the First Corinthians*, explains how to understand and practice the matters related with strife, evangelism, marriage, idolatry, and the spiritual gifts. You will be able to lead a more powerful Christian life if you find the right way by understanding your problem through the Word of God.

I give thanks to Geumsun Vin, the director of editorial bureau of Urim Books and all the staff, and I pray in the name of the Lord Jesus Christ that all the readers will clearly understand the will of God and practice it so that they can receive abundant blessings of God.

Jaerock Lee

Marriage · 221

Overview of the First Epistle to the Corinthians

1. About the Writer of the First Corinthians

The writer of the 1 Corinthians is the apostle Paul. Before believing in Jesus Christ his name was Saul. He was born in Tarsus of Cilicia and educated under Gamaliel. Gamaliel was a teacher of the Law who was highly respected by the public.

Since he studied under the best teacher of the time, Saul's knowledge of philosophy was excellent. He loved God very much and he very strictly kept the Law. One might say that he was the 'Hebrew of the Hebrews.' He was from the upper class and he was also a Roman citizen and had full citizenship of the Roman Empire.

Before he met the Lord Jesus, Saul persecuted the believers in the Lord. He thought the believers in Jesus were a threat to the Jewish religion and took the lead in persecuting and putting them in jail.

He met the Lord Jesus Christ on his way to Damascus. He was going there with the official document of the high priest to arrest those who were believers and followers of Jesus. Because God knew the love that Saul had for Him, He chose Saul to make him an apostle. God set him apart from the beginning of time because He knew that he would repent and become very faithful to the Lord Jesus if he could just meet Him.

Saul became known as 'Paul.' He worked faithfully, even to the point of death, as 'the apostle for the Gentiles'. He laid

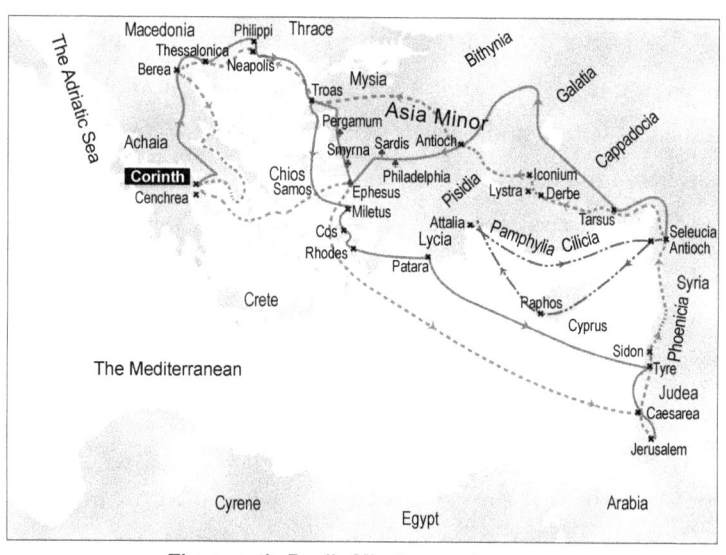

The apostle Paul's Missionary Journeys
(The first —·· , the second --- , the third —)

the foundation to spread the gospel to the ends of the earth through his three mission trips and established many churches in Asia Minor and Greece.

From the time he met the Lord, the apostle Paul dedicated himself for the Lord with all his life and completely fulfilled his duty as a servant of God and as an apostle.

2. Corinth

Corinth was a big city in southern part of Greece. At the time of Paul Corinth was ruled by the Roman Empire. It was adjacent to the sea on three sides; the east, west, and the south. Asia was its neighbor to the north, and Rome was to the west. Its location made it a center for trade between Asia and Rome.

It was a very busy and flourishing commercial city, which was crowded by government officers, soldiers, merchants, and sailors coming from various places in the Roman Empire. Many athletic events were frequently held, and it was also famous for its construction and arts. Naturally sensual cultures developed, and people were religiously and morally corrupted.

There were more than 30 temples of gentile gods including the temple of Aphrodite. People would perform rituals there before they went out merchandising. The city was so morally corrupted that there were more than a thousand prostitutes around the temple of Aphrodite.

3. Relation between the Church in Corinth and Apostle Paul

Around 50 AD, the apostle Paul preached the gospel in Corinth with Silas and Timothy during his second mission trip and established a church. He stayed at the house of Priscilla and Aquila and preached the gospel while making tents.

At first, he preached in the Jewish synagogues. But because of the opposition from the Jews, he stayed for a year and a half at the house of Titus Justus while he was laying the foundation of a church. The majority of the believers were gentiles, but there were also some Jews.

4. Time, Place, and Reason for Writing the Book

The book of 1 Corinthians is an epistle, or letter, that the apostle Paul wrote at Ephesus during this third mission trip, sometime around 55 AD. The believers in the church of Corinth were trying to live godly lives but they were faced with many problems because of the sensual and corrupt environment that surrounded them.

Conflicts arose between the rich and the poor believers, and there were also problems of law-suits between the believers. There were marital problems, problem maintaining chastity, and problems that arose in the eating of things that had been offered to idols. The apostle Paul wrote this letter to give them clear answers to such problems.

5. Distinctive Features of 1 Corinthians

The biblical books of Romans and Galatians are mostly concerned with issues of doctrine. But the First Epistle to the Corinthians deals mostly with practical problems of life. Among believers, 1 Corinthians is a practical answer book for problems that believers may face at personal levels or for the church in general.

It gives the clear answers for such issues as dissensions in the church, misuse of spiritual gifts, marriage, Holy Communion, 'food sacrificed to idols', and resurrection. Therefore, if we understand this book of 1 Corinthians clearly, it will be great help in our Christian life and we will be able to lead a blessed life by understanding the will of God clearly.

Chapter 1

PAUL BECAME AN APOSTLE IN THE PROVIDENCE OF GOD

— An Apostle and a Servant of God

— Salvation through God the Trinity

— For All to Agree

— Christ Is the Wisdom and Power of God

— Boast in the Lord

An Apostle
and a Servant of God

Paul, called as an apostle of Jesus Christ by the will of God, and Sosthenes our brother, (1:1)

The name of the apostle Paul before he met Jesus Christ was Saul. He arrested the disciples of the Lord and put them in jail. Saul was a strict legalist and to him it was blasphemy against God to follow Jesus as the Messiah.

It's the same with today's legalists. They interpret the Bible only literally. They pass judgment and condemnation on those who manifest powerful works of the Holy Spirit through the signs and wonders like those recorded in the early churches and they label such works as mysticism.

God knows everything. He knew that once Saul met Jesus he would repent and become a faithful worker of Jesus Christ. That is why he was chosen before the time began as the apostle for the Gentiles. Since he met the Lord on his way to Damascus, he became a faithful servant of God and dedicated his whole life to the Lord.

A servant is a person who is bound by his master and follows his master's will. The master in the church is God, and the servant who delivers the gospel has to obey the Word of God.

Five Different Kinds of Servants

In verse 1, Paul says he was 'called as an apostle of Jesus Christ by the will of God.' We cannot become an apostle by our will; we have to be called by the will of God.

Today, there are pastors who have become servants of God by the will of God, but there are others who have not. We can generally consider that there are five different groupings of pastors and servants of God.

The first are those who are called by God Himself. The second are those who have volunteered through the grace of God. The third are those who become pastors at the urging of others. The fourth are those who become pastors only as a job, and the fifth group is those who become pastors through the work of Satan.

Those Who Should Not Become Pastors

If one becomes a pastor by the urging of his parents or his

friends, problems may arise. For example, suppose one is not successful in his business ventures and things in general are not going well. Now suppose such a person goes to a prayer center and receives a prayer of prophecy from the pastor there that says, "You are chosen by God as His servant. That is why you will fail in all your attempts at business."

The person then responds, saying, "Can this really be so? I think you may be right because I have not succeeded in anything. Perhaps it is true that God didn't allow me to experience success in business so that He could make me His servant!"

Some people become pastors by the urging of some other people in this way. It's not because they love God. It's not right to become a pastor with fear and feeling forced to do it. In the Bible, we can see God called and used those who were intelligent and capable. He did not call those who failed in society and those who were incapable of accomplishing anything for themselves.

Also, some people become pastors only as a job thinking that as pastors they can spend the offerings at their discretion.

Furthermore, sometimes the enemy devil and Satan incite and motivate some people to become pastors for a variety of reasons. Satan disturbs the kingdom of God through such people.

Order in the Church

Many people question church order and hierarchy wondering, "If everyone in the church is equal in the sight of God, then why do we have to have different positions such as pastors, deacons, elders and so on?" We can understand that even in a family there is an order of authority. First are the family leaders, the father and mother, and then even among siblings there is an order among the brothers and sisters.

What if all family members acted in the place of the father? What if all employees in a company act like the CEO? Then, how can they achieve anything? Any group or organization must have an order of authority and management, and they must follow it so the organization can be maintained and operated.

1 Corinthians 12:28 says, *"And God has appointed in the church, first apostles, second prophets, third teachers, then miracles, then gifts of healings, helps, administrations, various kinds of tongues."* Therefore, in the order that is given we can see that those who have the gift of healing follow the apostles, prophets, teachers, and the miracles.

But today, some people just ignore this kind of order and cause problems. For example, when one receives the gift of healing, he does not use it for the glory of God following the order in the church, but becomes arrogant and looks down on the pastors and even passes judgment on some of them. Some people say they are prophesying and create divisions gathering people into one group or another. This kind of thing should not happen in the churches.

Who Is Qualified to Be Called an Apostle?

An apostle is somebody who does not have his own will, but fulfills his master or teacher's will completely. In other words, just as the Lord fulfilled the will of God completely, an apostle follows the way of the Lord completely. Therefore, there are many pastors, but not all of them are apostles.

How can we follow the will of God and fulfill it completely? Above all, we have to have the heart of the Lord and become sanctified. We can do what Jesus did only when, through the sanctification of heart, we receive the gift of healing, demonstrate the gift to perform the works of miracles, and use the gift of teaching. Then we can heal the sick, loosen the chains of injustice, and change the souls by the Word of God to give them the desire to live by God's will.

We see the word 'apostle' only after the Lord Jesus came. Then, who was Moses in the Old Testament? One may wonder who was greater. Was it Moses, or was it Paul, Sosthenes, and Timothy? Since they were apostles, were they greater than Moses?

If Moses had been born in the New Testament times, he would have been called an apostle, too. In the New Testament the Lord had disciples and taught them. Thus, all those who had the Lord as their teacher and fulfilled His will were apostles. But in the Old Testament, Moses did not have a teacher because he was taught by God Himself.

Figuratively, a king would not have a disciple. Likewise, in the Old Testament times, they received God's revelation directly, so the word 'apostle' was not necessary then. But in the New Testament, there were disciples of the Lord, and they were called the apostles.

John 14:12 says, *"Truly, truly, I say to you, he who believes in Me, the works that I do, he will do also; and greater works than these he will do; because I go to the Father."*

Therefore, true apostles pray fervently, receive God's power, and perform the powerful works just like the Lord did. They drive away the devil and heal the sick. They change people and motivate them to live in truth with the Word of God. If one fulfills the will of God completely this way, he can be called an apostle.

Salvation through God the Trinity

> To the church of God which is at Corinth, to those who have been sanctified in Christ Jesus, saints by calling, with all who in every place call on the name of our Lord Jesus Christ, their *Lord* and ours: Grace to you and peace from God our Father and the Lord Jesus Christ. (1:2-3)

Verse 2 says, "...those who have been sanctified in Christ Jesus." It refers to those who have cast off everything that is against the truth, who have clothed themselves with the truth, and who live in the truth. 'Saints' are those who have become sanctified in the truth. They are the ones who live according to the Word of God.

Those who do not live in the Word, are those who still commit sins. They are those who criticize, become jealous, and hate their brothers. They do not keep Sunday holy, so they may be 'churchgoers,' but as such, they cannot be called 'saints.' They are the chaff who cannot be saved in the sight of God.

The Lord will come to take the true wheat but not the chaff. So, we have to become the wheat. We have to continually strive to reach complete salvation by living in the Word of God.

In verse 3 the apostle Paul is blessing those who go to church and strive to become holy children of God. He blesses them to possess grace and peace. Even though they may not necessarily be qualified to be called saints, those who go to church and attend the worship services come to have faith. That is why he blesses all people with grace and peace.

Here, 'grace' refers to the salvation of Jesus Christ that God gives to us freely without any price that can be paid by us. God gives life to us and saves those of us who believe in the name of the Lord, that He died on the cross for us and He resurrected. This is His grace.

If we understand the truth of who God is, realize what His will is, know how we can receive blessings, and practice the Word of truth, then peace will come upon us. It is also God's blessing that He inspired Paul to write this book in the Bible.

I thank my God always concerning you for the grace of God which was given you in Christ Jesus, that in everything you were enriched in Him, in all speech and all knowledge, even as the testimony concerning Christ

was confirmed in you, so that you are not lacking in any gift, awaiting eagerly the revelation of our Lord Jesus Christ. (1:4-7)

The apostle Paul always says that he gives thanks to God. We who are saved through the grace of Jesus Christ should also make the same kind of confession.

There are people who say believers are good at making speeches, and yes, if we are armed with the truth, we will be good at speeches. But it's because of the Holy Spirit in our hearts that we may speak well, and not any ability of our own. So, even those with introverted character types can still boldly testify about Jesus Christ when they learn the Word of God.

Verse 6 says, "even as the testimony concerning Christ was confirmed in you." What was this testimony that Jesus Christ had that was confirmed in us? Jesus came to this earth as the Son of God and redeemed us from sins by dying on the cross. He fulfilled the will of God and resurrected. He later ascended into Heaven, but before His ascension He promised us that He would come back. As we listen to this Word of truth from pastors and brothers in faith, our faith grows and it is confirmed.

Jesus fulfilled the Law with love. We can also live in the Word of truth if we fully and completely love God. Those who keep the Word of God will also anxiously await the Second Coming of our bridegroom, Jesus Christ as in Revelation 22:20.

The Bible likens the Lord as to a bridegroom and believers to His brides. Thus, not only women, but all men as well, are referred to as the Lord's 'brides'. Those who have the gift of love, namely those who live in the truth, yearn and wait for the Lord our bridegroom, for they are preparing themselves as a bride would prepare.

Thus, verse 7 says, "so that you are not lacking in any gift, awaiting eagerly the revelation of our Lord Jesus Christ." Here the term 'gift' refers to the gift of love described in 1 Corinthians 13. It is the gift to love God with all our heart, mind, and soul.

He will also confirm you to the end, blameless in the day of our Lord Jesus Christ. God is faithful, through whom you were called into fellowship with His Son, Jesus Christ our Lord. (1:8-9)

Here, 'He', which refers to the Lord, refers to Jesus Christ and the Holy Spirit simultaneously. We cannot keep from living in sins without the help of the Holy Spirit. The Holy Spirit is given to us as a gift when we accept Jesus Christ. The Holy Spirit helps us to both understand the truth and to have the ability to live in the Word.

Verse 8 says, "He will also confirm you to the end, blameless in the day of our Lord Jesus Christ." The day of our Lord Jesus

Christ refers to the day of the Second Coming of Jesus Christ, or the Day of Judgment. 'You' in this verse refers to not only the members of the church in Corinth but all children of God.

We receive salvation in the name of Jesus Christ. Then, can we receive salvation only through Jesus Christ without God? Jesus Christ came to this earth through the love of God, and we are saved because Jesus Christ redeemed us from sins.

That doesn't mean we can be saved just with God and Jesus Christ. We cannot be saved if the Holy Spirit is not there for us. When we confess that we are sinners and humbly accept Jesus Christ as our Savior, the Holy Spirit comes into our heart and leads us to live in the truth. He lets us know about sin, righteousness, and judgment, and gives us grace and strength so that we can be firm in faith and receive salvation.

Therefore, we should understand that we are saved through God the Trinity, namely through the Father, the Son, and the Holy Spirit. Until the time of judgment, Jesus Christ and the Holy Spirit confirm us to make us blameless to the end.

Verse 9 says, "God is faithful, through whom you were called into fellowship with His Son, Jesus Christ our Lord." It says, 'you were called' because God called us to the church to believe in Jesus Christ. We didn't come before God on our own. Nobody can come to God unless the person is called by God. Therefore we should not say we came to church and have received salvation by our own initiative. We were called.

There are many expressions that refer to Jesus such as 'His Son,' 'Jesus,' 'Christ,' 'Our Lord,' etc. This is not because God likes complexity. It's because there are different spiritual meanings in each of those names.

God had a secret and a plan that He had hidden since before the time began. It was the plan for our salvation and the secret was Jesus Christ. When Jesus is referred to as 'His Son,' it means He is the only begotten Son of God. His Son came to this earth, as 'Jesus,' which means 'The one who will save His people from their sins' (Matthew 1:21).

'Christ' means 'The anointed One,' and this is the person who received a direct order from God. Namely, in the title 'His Son, Jesus Christ our Lord' it has the meaning 'the one and only Son of God, who is the secret hidden since before the time began, who was born on this earth to save His people from their sins, and He redeemed us from our sins and gave us salvation, thenceforth becoming our Savior.'

It also says God is faithful. It means God is trustworthy and truthful. Also, when we praise God, we say He is faithful. We praise His almightiness with this word. We can express God's beauty, loveliness, and mercy in general by saying that God is faithful.

For All to Agree

Now I exhort you, brethren, by the name of our Lord Jesus Christ, that you all agree and that there be no divisions among you, but that you be made complete in the same mind and in the same judgment. For I have been informed concerning you, my brethren, by Chloe's *people*, that there are quarrels among you. Now I mean this, that each one of you is saying, 'I am of Paul,' and 'I of Apollos,' and 'I of Cephas,' and 'I of Christ.' (1:10-12)

Paul urges all children of God to agree. But how can everyone agree since each one has different thoughts and standards? Here, 'for all to agree' means that we can do so when we understand the Word of God properly and live in the truth.

If there are quarrels, it means we still have thoughts of untruth and we are not united as one in God. Therefore, this word in essence means that we have to cast off untruthful thoughts and dwell in the truth.

If we live in the Word of God, our heart, will and thoughts will naturally become one. Our heart, mind, and soul, and will and thoughts can become one when we follow the voice of the Holy Spirit, because the truth is one.

For example, suppose a person is asking a multiple number of advisors for spiritual advice and guidance. Of course, individually the advisors won't all give a single answer that is the same. It's because they are not united as one in the truth. But if the advisors or the pastors arm themselves with the Word of God and hear the voice of the Holy Spirit clearly, they will all give almost the same answer.

As Romans 8:14 says, *"For all who are being led by the Spirit of God, these are sons of God,"* their answers can be the same because the Holy Spirit is guiding them.

The apostle Paul urges them by saying, "...that there be no divisions among you, but that you be made complete in the same mind and in the same judgment." We have to clothe ourselves with the Word of God alone, for the Word of God is the one truth and the one true standard of judgment.

Are you the kind of person who insists that you are right and causes dissensions and alienation among people? God calls such action to be a synagogue of Satan and does not forgive such a thing. There must never be dissension in the church.

Paul came to know that there was division in the church of

Corinth from Chloe's people. The members in the church of Corinth followed their own thoughts and did not stand in the truth. This caused divisions among them. That is why they were saying "I am of Paul" or "I am of Apollos."

Today, we often see divisions in churches. This is not done by the inspiration of the Holy Spirit, but through the instigation of Satan. If anyone causes division because his thoughts do not agree with God's Word, then it is a synagogue of Satan.

Once I went to a certain place to lead a revival meeting there. There were about 40 churches in that area. I heard that many churches had multiple factions within them. Because of them the pastors were not able to stay for very long serving there. I was very sorry to hear such a thing. There was even a law-suit among them because each one was trying to become the leader. This kind of thing comes from Satan.

In Matthew 16:21, Jesus said to His disciples that He must go to Jerusalem, and suffer many things from the elders and chief priests and scribes, and be killed, and be raised up on the third day.

Hearing this Peter said that it should never happen to the Lord. He said it because he loved his master. But Jesus said, "Get behind Me, Satan," because it was the will of God for Him to take the sufferings of the cross and it was for the fulfillment of the providence of salvation.

Of course, Jesus didn't mean Peter was Satan. He said it because Peter was having a fleshly thought. Peter's words were not from the Holy Spirit but they came through the works of Satan.

For us to become God's beloved children, we should never slander or criticize others and cause dissensions to arise. We have to have one heart and one will in the Lord with fear and love for God. We should also love our neighbors as ourselves, praying for them with tears.

Verse 12 says, "Now I mean this, that each one of you is saying, 'I am of Paul,' and 'I of Apollos,' and 'I of Cephas,' and 'I of Christ.'"

How can there be divisions in the church? It was not pastors and elders of the church who redeemed us from sins by dying on the cross. Everyone belongs to Jesus Christ because Jesus was crucified to redeem all mankind from sins. It should never be said that we are of any pastor, elder, or anyone else but the Lord Jesus Christ.

Therefore, we should not say, "I was offended because of that believer, and that's why I am not attending church." We attend church looking up to Jesus Christ only, and thus we should not stumble because of men. Also, those who get angry do so because they are narrow-minded. Those with broad hearts will not be short-tempered because they can accept and embrace others. If anybody is criticizing, passing judgment on others, is short-tempered, or causes divisions, then he should look back humbly on himself.

In doing this we can then have the determination to cast off the things that are against the Word of God, put our trust in His Word and obey Him. We can then be in God's love.

Has Christ been divided? Paul was not crucified for you, was he? Or were you baptized in the name of Paul? I thank God that I baptized none of you except Crispus and Gaius, so that no one would say you were baptized in my name. (1:13-15)

Paul said, "Has Christ been divided?" He felt very sorry for the divisions in the church of Corinth. He was rather thankful that he baptized only a few of the members there, for some believers in the church of Corinth misunderstood that they were saved through the person who baptized them.

Paul taught them with the truth, but they had the misunderstanding of thinking that Paul was giving them salvation. How embarrassed Paul must have been! So, had he baptized more believers then they would have served him like he was the Savior. That is why he was thankful that he baptized only a few of them.

Pastors or servants of God can only lead the people to the side of God by teaching them that Jesus Christ is the Savior. They can never give salvation. As said in 1 Corinthians 3:6, men can only plant and water, and the One who makes it grow is God alone.

Only Jesus Christ is the Savior. Some people asked following question. "Pastor, isn't it wrong for the believers to follow you like Jesus?" Then, I answer. "No, none of my church members think of me as the Savior. They follow me only as a servant of the Lord with whom God shows His works." In fact, I feel very embarrassed to receive such a question in the first place. I can understand how Paul must have felt when he was writing this part.

Today, there are some people who claim that they are the 'Savior' or the 'Olive Tree,' and also there are those who follow them. It's such a pity!

If I say, "I am God, so follow me!" there are none of my church members who would believe it, for they are well equipped with the truth of God.

To love a servant of God whom God loves is to love the church, and to love the church is to love God. Because we love God, we love the servant of God who guides us to salvation. If we say we love God without loving the pastor who is seen, then, it is a lie.

All want their parents to be respectable and the best possible people they can be. If the children don't trust their parents, it is likely that they will go astray. If we do not trust the pastor who is leading us, it's difficult for us to dedicate ourselves for the church.

Then, we will naturally distance ourselves from the church, not loving God. If the pastor of a church cannot be respected, it's something very unfortunate.

Now I did baptize also the household of Stephanas; beyond that, I do not know whether I baptized any other. (1:16)

Paul said that he had baptized only Crispus and Gaius in Corinth. Here, he says he also baptized the household of Stephanas. He baptized them in Achaia on his mission trip.

1 Corinthians 16:15-18 says, *"Now I urge you, brethren (you know the household of Stephanas, that they were the first fruits of Achaia, and that they have devoted themselves for ministry to the saints), that you also be in subjection to such men and to everyone who helps in the work and labors. I rejoice over the coming of Stephanas and Fortunatus and Achaicus, because they have supplied what was lacking on your part. For they have refreshed my spirit and yours. Therefore acknowledge such men."*

Stephanas was a very faithful person who devoted himself for ministry to the saints, and the apostle Paul himself baptized him. Paul then urged others to acknowledge such men. He also urged them to obey not only such men who devoted themselves to serve the believers but also everyone who helped in the service and works.

In this world, people obey those who have higher positions or greater authority. But Christians should not look at the social status, authority or wealth. We should consider it a noble attribute to obey those who are faithful in the Lord, for we don't consider social status, authority, or wealth as something important in the Lord.

We should think how obedient we are to those men of faith who devote their lives for the ministry. We should look back on whether or not we spoke carelessly of them or passed judgment on such people. The apostle Paul urged the people of Corinth to acknowledge those who are faithful in the Lord and let others know about how they respected them and the work they were doing.

In verse 16 apostle Paul says, "Now I did baptize also the household of Stephanas; beyond that, I do not know whether I baptized any other." He made such a remark because his memory was somewhat dimmed after so long on the mission trips.

Then, did apostle Paul baptize only those three people? In Acts 16:33, when the apostle Paul and Silas were in prison, the jailor and his household accepted the Lord and were baptized by Paul. It's just a case of Paul's memory not being clear about it by then.

> **For Christ did not send me to baptize, but to preach the gospel, not in cleverness of speech, so that the cross of Christ would not be made void. (1:17)**

God does not appoint His servants and allow them to stand on the pulpit for them to focus on baptism. It is done to let them preach the message of the cross and the gospel so that the people will receive salvation.

Everyone has different levels in the use of words. Some have extensive knowledge while others have good oratory skills for public speaking. That is why they may preach with words of knowledge or impart some deep philosophical thoughts. But the apostle Paul did not preach the gospel with the knowledge of this world or the cleverness of speech.

Some say they cannot spread the gospel because they don't have the wisdom of words. Even though the preacher may not have good speaking skills, the works of the Holy Spirit will take place when they preach who God is, who Jesus Christ is, and the way of the cross, the resurrection, the Second Coming of the Lord, and about Heaven and Hell.

As the days go by, people have more knowledge and education, but they don't live a morally better life. Rather they become stained with sins more quickly. We cannot change the hearts of men or plant faith in them with the cleverness of speech or the knowledge of this world.

That is why verse 17 says, "...not in cleverness of speech, so that the cross of Christ would not be made void." To preach the gospel with the knowledge of the world or cleverness of speech is not in agreement with God's will, and thus Holy Spirit cannot work through them.

God is spirit, and His Word is also the word of the fourth dimension, which is a spiritual dimension. 1 Corinthians 2:13 says, *"Which things we also speak, not in words taught by human wisdom, but in those taught by the Spirit, combining spiritual thoughts with spiritual words."* We cannot understand the Word of God without the help of the Holy Spirit.

Exodus 12:8-9 talks about how to eat the lamb. It says, *"They shall eat the flesh that same night, roasted with fire, and they shall eat it with unleavened bread and bitter herbs. Do not eat any of it raw or boiled at all with water, but rather roasted with fire, both its head and its legs along with its entrails."*

The lamb in Exodus spiritually refers to Jesus Christ. John 1:29 recorded, *"Behold, the Lamb of God who takes away the sin of the world!"* Unless we eat the flesh and drink the blood of the Son of Man, we do not have life and we cannot gain eternal life (John 6:53). Therefore, we have to eat the flesh of the Son of Man, which is the body of the Lord, who is the Lamb.

Then, how can we eat the Lamb? It tells us that we must not eat it raw, or boil it, but roast it over fire, all of it including its head, legs, and entrails. This means that we have to understand the Words in all sixty-six books of the Bible through the inspiration of the Holy Spirit. Eating the Lamb raw or boiled in water symbolizes understanding the Word of God literally and mixing it with the knowledge of the world such as philosophy.

Let us realize that we cannot change the hearts of men or plant faith in them with just cleverness of speech. We should preach the gospel only by following the inspiration of the Holy Spirit.

Christ is the Wisdom and Power of God

For the word of the cross is to those who are perishing foolishness, but to us who are being saved it is the power of God. (1:18)

For those who are perishing, namely for those who do not believe in Jesus Christ, the word of the cross seems foolish.

Some unbelievers consider believers to be foolish. Some others believe only in themselves saying, "How can we believe in God when He can't be seen?" It's because the message of the cross seems foolish to them. But for believers who are receiving salvation, it is the power of God.

John 11:25-26 says, *"Jesus said to her, 'I am the resurrection and the life; he who believes in Me will live even if he dies, and everyone who lives and believes in Me will never die. Do you believe this?'"*

As spoken, those children of God who have accepted Jesus Christ will never die. Their physical bodies will die and go back to dust, but their spirit will be saved and live forever in the kingdom of Heaven. That is why the Bible says, when the believers die, that they are said to be "asleep", not "dead".

Acts 7:59-60 says, *"They went on stoning Stephen as he called on the Lord and said, 'Lord Jesus, receive my spirit!' Then falling on his knees, he cried out with a loud voice, 'Lord, do not hold this sin against them!' Having said this, he fell asleep."* Those who die after accepting the Lord will be resurrected like the Lord was resurrected. That's why the Bible says he "fell asleep."

Coming out of death to resurrection and eternal life cannot be understood or even imagined with the knowledge of men. It is done only by the power of God.

Then, what is the power of God?

John 8:44 says, *"You are of your father the devil, and you want to do the desires of your father."* This does not mean our physical father is the devil but that those who do not belong to God belong to the devil, the ruler of this world.

Until Jesus Christ took the cross on the behalf of us sinners, we all formerly belonged to the devil. But through the way of the cross, God has become our Father. This is the power of God.

1 John 3:10 says, *"By this the children of God and the*

children of the devil are obvious: anyone who does not practice righteousness is not of God, nor the one who does not love his brother."

It says those who do not love their brothers do not belong to God. If they don't belong to God then they must belong to the devil. At one time we all belonged to the devil. None of us truly loved our brothers living in righteousness. We came to love our brothers and live in righteousness only after we listened to the way of the cross, accepted Jesus Christ, and came to live in the Word of God.

It is in this way that those who once belonged to the devil come to belong to God. This is the power of God. We had no choice but to live in sin before, but from the moment we accept Jesus Christ, the Holy Spirit comes into us and makes it possible for us to cast off all forms of unrighteousness and live in the righteousness of God. This is the power of God.

When we were in the world, not believing in God, it wasn't easy for us to quit such things as smoking and drinking. The self-determination at times doesn't even last for three days. I also tried to quit smoking. I threw away all the cigarettes I had, but I had to pick them up again and start to smoke again after a couple of days.

But after I accepted the Lord, it was so easy to quit smoking and drinking. I could quit both of them immediately because I was full of the Holy Spirit through prayers. It is the power of God to change people and enable them to cast away untruth and live in righteousness by the help of the Holy Spirit.

For it is written, "I will destroy the wisdom of the wise, and the cleverness of the clever I will set aside." (1:19)

In this world, there are some groups of people who claim to be wise and intellectually advanced. They claim to be fore-most in their educational systems, advancements in medical science, scientific and technological development and even aspects of their cultures. But before God and for the believers, it is not so.

Ecclesiastes 1:2 says, *"'Vanity of vanities,' says the Preacher, 'Vanity of vanities! All is vanity.'"* Knowledge, fame, social power, and wealth all perish and disappear. All men are destined to die. We cannot receive salvation and go to the heavenly kingdom through our wealth, wisdom, or intellect. The leader of a country may possess and enjoy many things, but, in the end he too will fall into Hell if he has no faith. So what is the use of his wealth, wisdom and intellectual abilities?

Therefore, God says He will destroy the wisdom of the wise and set aside the cleverness of the clever. Even these things will finally perish and thus they are valueless. In the sight of God, they are in fact very foolish.

However, it is not valueless to have fame, social power, or wealth in Jesus Christ. We can give glory to God by offering these qualities for furthering the kingdom and righteousness of God. This will be our reward in Heaven, and thus it is a blessing.

Those who don't have faith do not know about the Creator God who made them. They just consider their knowledge, wealth and wisdom of greatest value and go the way of destruction. Thus, in the sight of God, they are very foolish.

Isaiah 29:14 says, *"Therefore behold, I will once again deal marvelously with this people, wondrously marvelous; and the wisdom of their wise men will perish, and the discernment of their discerning men will be concealed."*

This Word was fulfilled through Jesus Christ. In Matthew 11:25-26 it says, *"At that time Jesus said, 'I praise You, Father, Lord of heaven and earth, that You have hidden these things from the wise and intelligent and have revealed them to infants. Yes, Father, for this way was well-pleasing in Your sight.'"*

Those who think that they are wise cannot accept Jesus Christ and receive salvation, but those who are humble like children will believe in Jesus Christ and receive salvation. Therefore, the truth is that those who say they are wise are actually foolish and their discernment is obscured.

Those who considered themselves to be wise did not accept Jesus. Their wisdom and knowledge obscured their discernment of the truth and they were foolish. That is why the scribes and teachers of the law who thought they knew the Word of God very well crucified their Messiah. They went the way of destruction, and it means they had no wisdom or understanding.

Then, do we have to forsake all kinds of knowledge and wisdom? I am not saying that the knowledge and wisdom a person gains are bad. However, we must be able to use them for God. Everything we do under the sun is vanity, and thus we first have to have the knowledge and wisdom of knowing God.

Where is the wise man? Where is the scribe? Where is the debater of this age? Has not God made foolish the wisdom of the world? (1:20)

To fear God is the origin of knowledge and wisdom (Proverbs 1:7, 9:10). In the sight of God, the standard to distinguish whether or not we have wisdom is whether or not we fear God.

We can gain true life only when we receive wisdom and knowledge given by God from above. God is emphasizing this point. If we go the way of destruction because of the knowledge of this world, how foolish it is to have worldly knowledge! Thus, only the Word of truth in the reverent fear of God can be the only standard of judgment. Those who are foolish despise His wisdom and teachings and do not accept the Word of God.

True scribes are those who understand the Word of the truth and make their spiritual bread of it. Even good speech is meaningless unless it has life in it. We can be true debaters only when we are armed with the Word of God and make a speech. God is asking a question of those people who are going the way of destruction: "You people, where are your wisdom and understanding? Where are scribes and debaters?" Then He states, "Even though they boast of their knowledge and wisdom, they cannot be saved, and they cannot experience the power of God." In conclusion it says, "Thus, Has God not made foolish the wisdom of the world?"

> For since, in the wisdom of God the world, through its wisdom, did not *come to* know God, God was well-pleased through the foolishness of the message preached to save those who believe. (1:21)

Men think they have wisdom but they cannot know God with man's wisdom alone. That is why God lets many people reach salvation through preaching.

God's wisdom is endless, but the knowledge and wisdom of this world prevent us from believing in the power of God, and thus, it is foolish in the sight of God. We cannot understand the Creator God with man's wisdom and knowledge, and that is why God was well-pleased through the foolishness of the message preached to save those who believe.

John 20:29 says, *"Blessed are they who did not see, and yet believed."* Usually, people first come to believe in God through hearing the Word of God preached. Faith is the substance of the things hoped for and the evidences of things not seen. It can create something out of nothing.

God is pleased to save men through this faith itself, because

He can gain true children who love Him from the depth of their hearts.

Those who are arrogant and stiff-necked say they have wisdom. But God looks for good-hearted people who have pure hearts like children to accept the gospel. Thus, He is well-pleased by the foolishness of the message preached to save those who believe.

For indeed Jews ask for signs and Greeks search for wisdom; (1:22)

Here, the 'Jews' has two meanings.

First, it refers to the hypocrites among the Israelites who say they know God, but still ask for signs of evidence.

At the time of Jesus, the Jews did not recognize their Savior even when He stood before their eyes. It's because they were seeking signs. They wanted the Messiah to appear in a glorious and magnified manner. They expected the Messiah to set them free from the Roman Empire, and rule over them.

But the real Messiah who was preaching the gospel to them was not dignified at all. He was born in a stable; He never wore any fancy clothes; He didn't even have a place to stay and slept in the wilderness or in the mountains; He couldn't even eat well. He totally looked like an unimportant person. Those hypocrites who were seeking signs, only sought the things seen in their eyes, and they couldn't recognize the Messiah.

Jesus having been born in a stable also has a spiritual meaning. Ecclesiastes 3:18 says, *"I said to myself concerning the sons of men, 'God has surely tested them in order for them to see that men's all is vanity and that they are no better than beasts.'"* Jesus was born in a stable where animals live in order to redeem men who are no different from beasts and recover them to have the original image created by God.

But the hypocrites who were seeking signs could not understand this deep and profound providence. They couldn't see spiritual things. They only tried to find the Messiah in their own thoughts following the lust of the flesh, the lust of the eyes, and the boastful pride of this life. Eventually, they couldn't even recognize the Messiah who was right before their eyes.

The second meaning of the term 'Jews' spiritually means 'believers.' But the Jews whom Paul is giving advice are not the Jews with spiritual meaning of believer, but those Jews who were hypocrites.

It says the Jews ask for signs. What does the Word of God say about seeing and believing? John 20:29 says, *"Jesus said to him, 'Because you have seen Me, have you believed? Blessed are they who did not see, and yet believed.'"* Blessed are those who believe in God and accept Jesus Christ and the kingdom of Heaven just by hearing the Word of God and not seeking signs to confirm their belief.

Some say they will believe only when they see it with their own eyes. But when they do actually see the manifestation of the works of God, will they really believe? Most people who say this will not believe in and accept God even when they see the evidence of the living God through His signs and wonders. They may believe for that moment, but sooner or later they will forsake their faith. But those who can believe without seeing do not have such shaky hearts, and in this way they are truly the blessed ones.

Paul said that the Jews ask for signs and the Greeks search for wisdom. Why would Greeks search for wisdom? The Greeks were knowledgeable and cultured. Greek philosophy was well advanced early in their history. The people also possessed wisdom. They studied to develop and advance their knowledge and culture and to live happier lives.

Because Greece had such wisdom and knowledge, Paul mentioned the Greeks when he was talking about wisdom. "The Greeks search for wisdom" means that those who have knowledge and wisdom will continue to learn and seek more wisdom.

...but we preach Christ crucified; to Jews, a stumbling block, and to Gentiles, foolishness. (1:23)

It is not 'Jews' or 'Greeks', but the true children of God who testify to the cross of Jesus Christ. They don't talk about how to earn more money, gain more fame, or enjoy social power. They focus on how to receive salvation and the cross of the Christ.

The Jews who were hypocritical in belief did not like this. It's because the kind of Messiah that the Jews wanted was not one who had been crucified.

Even today, when we testify to Jesus Christ, some people say they will believe if they can see Him and touch Him. With hardened hearts, they ask for signs and say they cannot believe unless they see. These people pile up sins upon sins. If we preach Jesus Christ and tell them to repent, it becomes a stumbling block to them.

Nevertheless, in one corner of their hearts, they cannot deny that God exists. There is still some good conscience left in the depths of their hearts. That is why they become fearful when they hear about Heaven and Hell. So, then, they should repent and seek God, but they just don't want to listen such a thing and try to repel their fears.

Also, the passage in verse 23 says the preaching of the Christ crucified is foolishness to the Gentiles. Gentiles refer to all unbelievers whether Jews or Greeks. To all those who do not believe, the message of the Christ crucified seems foolish.

While spreading the gospel, if we say, "God is living. Incurable diseases were healed by the prayer in the church," then, many people consider the preachers foolish thinking such works cannot happen and they must have been some kind of coincidence. It's because they cannot understand it with their wisdom and knowledge.

With the wisdom and knowledge of the world, we cannot

believe creation from nothingness. But God certainly created things out of nothing. When He said, "Let there be light," light came to exist. He created the sun, the moon, the stars and all things in the universe with His Word (Genesis 1:3-31). Also, He says, "All things are possible to him who believes," and we can see Him at work according to our faith.

In my church, we can see that so many different kinds of incurable diseases are healed when they receive prayer with faith. It's not something that has happened just a couple of times, but the church members always experience such works.

Some people who consider themselves wise say about such works: "Those illnesses may have been healed through mind-over matter and mental power together with the assurance that they can be healed." But even two or three-year-old babies receive healing through prayer, and what kind of knowledge do they have that they can be healed through mental power? With men's knowledge or wisdom, we can neither meet God nor go the way of eternal life.

Some unbelievers may persecute the believers around them saying, "Does the church provide you with food or what?" Of course, the church provides them with food. The church provides spiritual bread which is the Word of God. God's Word is living and it leads us to eternal life, and therefore, this Word is the true bread that does not decay.

But the worldly people just look at the visible and fleshly

things of the world and ask such questions. But the children of God can boldly testify to the Lord for they know what the truth is.

> **...but to those who are the called, both Jews and Greeks, Christ [is] the power of God and the wisdom of God. (1:24)**

Christ is the power of God to those children of God who believe in Him, whether they are Jews or Greeks.

Even among the hypocritical Jews, some of them believed in Jesus Christ and received salvation. Also, there were some Greeks who met God while they were seeking knowledge and wisdom. Not everyone who has knowledge denies God. Some people seek God and meet Him because of the knowledge they gain.

Once, we knew nothing about being resurrected or about eternal life. We just thought our earthly existence was everything. But since we have come to know Jesus Christ and accept Him, we can believe in God, who can revive the dead, and we can believe Heaven and Hell actually exist.

When we accept Jesus Christ, our dead spirit is revived, and we can go the way of eternal life. As Jesus said, He is the way, the truth, and the life. He is the Christ who gives us life and becomes the way to the kingdom of Heaven, and thus He is the power of God.

The passage also says the Christ is not just the power of God but also the wisdom of God. Because He saves us, allows for us to become perfect, and gives us eternal life, He is wisdom.

Who in this world can give us salvation and change our lives? Who can change the heart of an evil man into a good heart? It's possible only by the power of God. That is why verse 24 says that Christ is "the power and wisdom of God" to both Jews and Greeks.

Because the foolishness of God is wiser than men, and the weakness of God is stronger than men. (1:25)

The foolishness of God is something that looks foolish in the sight of the unbelievers. In fact, there is no foolishness in God.

Jesus told us to turn the other cheek when somebody strikes one of our cheeks. In this world, if a person is struck without any reason, he thinks it is right to strike back. Worldly people even tend to think that not striking back is cowardly. Jesus tells us to give the tunic when somebody asks for our outer garment, which is like surrendering your underclothes if someone asks for your shirt and pants! Then, does that mean we have to go around naked?

With the value system and viewpoint of the world, God's Word seems foolish. But this Word brings us love and peace, and it is the way of victory. We can even love our enemies and they will be moved when we act by the Word of God (1 Samuel 24:16-21). This is the way to have love and peace and victory.

Also, it says, "Weakness of God is stronger than men." Does God have weakness? For the believers, God has no weakness at all. But in the sight of the unbelievers, God may seem weak.

It's because the truth tells us to yield, give way, endure, and even step back in an attempt to have peace, and this may seem cowardly in the viewpoint of the world. The people in the world try to take more and flaunt themselves to be noticed more, but the instruction of God's Word is the opposite.

Jesus was also weak. He didn't quarrel or cry out. He was rather mild and meek, so in the eyes of the worldly people, Jesus was considered to be weak. Matthew 12:19-20 describes Jesus' character very well. It reads: *"He will not quarrel, nor cry out; nor will anyone hear His voice in the streets. A battered reed He will not break off, and a smoldering wick He will not put out, until He leads justice to victory."*

Because Jesus became weak as above, He finally broke the authority of death and resurrected to fulfill the will of God. That is why the passage is saying weakness is power.

Boast in the Lord

For consider your calling, brethren, that there
were not many wise according to the flesh, not many
mighty, not many noble; (1:26)

This verse tells us how God calls us.

'According to the flesh' refers to unbelievers. Those who
do not believe in God boast of themselves saying they have
fame, money, wisdom, knowledge, good educations, good
families, good speaking skills, and so on, but all those things are
foolishness to God.

What is the use of boasting of their education, wisdom,
family background, or money while they are going the way
of death and they do not know God? It is foolish because
eventually all those things will perish.

...but God has chosen the foolish things of the world

to shame the wise, and God has chosen the weak things of the world to shame the things which are strong, and the base things of the world and the despised God has chosen, the things that are not, so that He may nullify the things that are, so that no man may boast before God. (1:27-29)

'The wise' refers to those who call themselves wise. But they are not wise in the sight of God. In Proverbs 1:7 and 9:10 we find that the fear of the LORD is the beginning of wisdom. The verses tell us that God chooses the foolish of the world to shame the wise.

Those children of God who have accepted Jesus Christ receive salvation and enjoy an eternal and a joyous life in the kingdom of Heaven. But, those who do not know or seek God and think they are wise, will eventually fall into Hell. They will all be ashamed.

In Luke 16 we read about the rich man and the beggar Lazarus. There was a rich man, and he habitually dressed in purple and fine linen. He lived a joyous life in splendor every day. A poor man named Lazarus laid at his gate. He was covered with sores and he longed to be fed with the crumbs which were falling from the rich man's table. Dogs were even coming and licking his sores.

Lazarus died and was carried away by angels to Abraham's bosom. The rich man also died. In Hades he lifted up his eyes in torment and saw Abraham far away and Lazarus at his bosom. He cried out and said, "Father Abraham, have mercy on me, and send Lazarus so that he may dip the tip of his finger in water and cool off my tongue, for I am in agony in this flame." But he couldn't be helped.

The rich man loved the world and the worldly pleasures, but he would not love God. After his death, he went into the Lower Hades and remained there in pain. But the poor man, Lazarus, though he lived in poverty, feared God. He received salvation and went to the bosom of Abraham.

The rich man thought he was wise while he was living on earth. But after his death, the beggar Lazarus, who seemed foolish on earth, was enjoying happiness. The rich man had to suffer in the flames. It was not just for one or two days, but forever. How shameful it is for him! We must be grateful to God for He has chosen us and we could have become His children.

Verse 27 says, "but God has chosen the foolish things of the world to shame the wise, and God has chosen the weak things of the world to shame the things which are strong." If God calls you and chooses you, you are truly blessed. It is a greater honor to be recognized by God and become a deacon, deaconess, or an elder and receive duties in the church than to be recognized by the leaders of countries and nations.

Then, why does God choose the foolish and not the wise? Jesus said, *"Truly I say to you, unless you are converted and become like children, you will not enter the kingdom of heaven"* (Matthew 18:3).

Spiritual children are simple, pure, and humble. They simply accept the Word of truth like children, believe it, and they obey it. So, they can change and reach the kingdom of Heaven.

But those who think they are wise in this world will consider those who have hearts like children to be foolish. But God chooses and uses those who have simple and good hearts. He chooses those who are poor in heart.

Our next verse says, "God has chosen the weak things of the world to shame the things which are strong." Jesus is the Son of God, but He was also very weak according to worldly standards. If somebody struck Him on the right cheek, He would turn the other as well. He would not even break off a bruised reed. What a weak person He seemed to be!

This 'weak' Jesus was crucified, and this 'weak' Jesus resurrected and ascended into Heaven to become the King of kings and the Lord of lords! In contrast, those who were strong and who persecuted Jesus went the way of destruction. Thus, God shamed the strong by the weak.

Verse 28 says, "and the base things of the world and the despised God has chosen, the things that are not, so that He may nullify the things that are." Peter, one of the disciples of Jesus, was a fisherman. As an occupation, it was not one that was respected very much. But God chose these lowly people to nullify and shame those who were lifted up among men.

In Acts 4:13-14 it tells us more about the status of the disciples, *"Now as they observed the confidence of Peter and John and understood that they were uneducated and untrained men, they were amazed, and began to recognize them as having been with Jesus. And seeing the man who had been healed standing with them, they had nothing to say in reply."*

People thought they were uneducated and foolish. But as they accepted Jesus Christ, received the Holy Spirit, and changed completely, people were surprised. Acts 2:43-44 says, *"Everyone kept feeling a sense of awe; and many wonders and signs were taking place through the apostles. All those who had believed were together and had all things in common."*

The disciples of the Lord were called from fisherman and from among minorities who were despised in this world. Jesus chose these people and used them. The worldly people came to be afraid of them. On the outside, they denied the powerful signs and wonders manifested by the disciples, but they still had some conscience left in their hearts. So, when they saw the things manifested that they couldn't do, they were afraid.

Verse 29 says, "...so that no man may boast before God." If God calls and uses those who have much wisdom, wealth, education, or money in this world, will they have reverent fear of God?

People like these say they are successful in this world because they are well-educated and smart, not because God blessed them. Also, if these people pastor a church and are successful they are likely to think it is because they are wise and well-educated. They think they are excellent and capable at what they do. They do not give all the glory to God.

That is why God chooses those who are foolish, weak, and despised so that they will not boast of themselves or lift themselves up. We know the truth, and we have to rely on God and acknowledge His guidance in all things. We should be able to profess in everything that it is only in Him that all things are possible.

But by His doing you are in Christ Jesus, who became to us wisdom from God, and righteousness and sanctification, and redemption, (1:30)

All men and all things in the universe were from God. God established Adam as the lord of all creatures. But Adam was cursed due to his sin and all the things that he had authority over were also cursed. All authority that he had was handed over to the devil.

That is why Luke 4:5-6 says, *"And [the devil] led Him up and showed Him all the kingdoms of the world in a moment of time. And the devil said to Him, 'I will give You all this domain and its glory; for it has been handed over to me, and I give it to whomever I wish.'"*

The cursed world did not look good like it did when it was

first created by God. God sent His one and only Son, Jesus, to this earth to save the cursed mankind from the hands of the enemy devil.

God has shown us such great love; the sinless Jesus died on the cross taking the sins of all men, so that anyone who believes in Him can receive eternal life and become God's children. As we become God's children again, we are of God and in Jesus Christ.

Then, what does it mean by, "Christ Jesus, who became to us wisdom from God, and righteousness and sanctification, and redemption"?

Wisdom is to fear God. God's wisdom saves us, leads us to cast off sins, allows for us to live in the truth, and guides us to the eternal kingdom of Heaven.

Along with this wisdom, Jesus Christ gave us righteousness, sanctification, and redemption. Here, righteousness is goodness, and this goodness is the Word of God. When we accept Jesus Christ, we will live in goodness and righteousness following the Word.

This fruit of righteousness is seen in sanctification. When we take the Word in our heart as spiritual bread, it will show in action. That is why 1 John 3:18 says, *"Little children, let us not love with word or with tongue, but in deed and truth."*

We become united as one and redeemed in the Lord who is the way, truth, and life. We should not be bound by the world but redeemed by Jesus Christ.

...so that, just as it is written, "Let him who boasts, boast in the Lord." (1:31)

Why does God choose the foolish, the weak, and the despised of the world to do His work? It is to, "Let him who boasts, boast in the Lord." What can we boast of in our lives? Unbelievers may boast of many things, such as money, fame, social power, knowledge, and wisdom.

Ecclesiastes 1:2-3 says, *" 'Vanity of vanities,' says the Preacher, 'Vanity of vanities! All is vanity.' "* What advantage does man have in all his work which he does under the sun?" Therefore, there is nothing but the Lord to boast. Everything outside the Lord is in vain, since even the best things will eventually perish and they will only lead us to Hell.

We who know this must boast only in the Lord. Only what we do in the Lord is not in vain. Whether we study, run a business, or eat or drink or whatever we do, we should try to give glory to God in all things in the truth. To live this way is a truly blessed life. This kind of life is not in vain because God is well-pleased with it, and it will give us heavenly rewards.

Chapter 2

GOD'S WISDOM

— The Manifestation of Power through
  the Spirit
— The Way of the Cross,
  the Wisdom of God
— God's Grace Understood through
  the Holy Spirit
— Spiritual Things Are Discerned
  through the Spirit

The Manifestation of Power through the Spirit

And when I came to you, brethren, I did not come
with superiority of speech or of wisdom, proclaiming
to you the testimony of God. For I determined to
know nothing among you except Jesus Christ, and
Him crucified. (2:1-2)

The apostle Paul was a highly educated man with vast
knowledge. But he didn't depend on his education or
knowledge. He didn't rely on superior speaking ability or his
wisdom when he was delivering the message of God. This is the
will of God.

We cannot save souls through eloquent speech, persuasive
argument, or the wisdom of men. That is why we should be
careful when we read books about faith. We shouldn't accept
something just because it is in a book written by a famous
person.

If an author who prays a lot and has deep communication with God writes a book, then it is very likely the book will be beneficial. But even though the author may be well educated and knowledgeable, if he is not a man of prayer and fasting and does not communicate with God, it is very likely that those books won't be very beneficial. It is because the book was written with only the author's personal knowledge and wisdom.

To what did Paul attest? He only testified to Jesus Christ and that He was crucified on the cross. This is what a servant of God is supposed to do. A servant has to testify to who Jesus Christ is, why He had to come to this earth, why He was crucified, and how He redeemed us from our sins. He also has to preach about His resurrection and Second Coming so that God's children can have their hope in Heaven while living their lives on earth.

That is why the apostle Paul says he determined to know nothing except these things. From the time he met the Lord, he understood that his knowledge was not a benefit but it was a hindrance in saving souls.

When men have gained much knowledge and have developed science and technology well, they become arrogant and they are likely to say that there is no God. Those who search for the knowledge of this world do not seek God. That is why the apostle Paul says that he was determined to know nothing 'except Jesus Christ, and Him crucified.'

Therefore, those who want to become pastors or work for

God must read the Bible rather than reading books written by men who write with their own wisdom and knowledge. Also, they have to pray to have spiritual communication with God and strive to receive the power of God. This is the only way to save souls and enlarge the kingdom of God.

In Ephesians 5:16 the apostle Paul urges them *"[to] make the most of your time, because the days are evil."* We have to have the communication with God and save many dying souls in this evil generation. We have to testify to the living God and lead them to faith. Furthermore, we have to remember that these things are not done through the knowledge of this world.

I was with you in weakness and in fear and in much trembling, (2:3)

Before he met the Lord, the apostle Paul had no fear. He stood in the forefront in arresting and persecuting the believers of Jesus Christ. But from the time he met the Lord, he was with the people in their weakness, in their fear, and in their trembling.

What does this mean? If we truly believe and know God, His workers should show their weakness before God and before other believers. The only strong one is God, and we have to understand that we cannot do anything unless He is with us.

Some say they have the ability to speak well because of their knowledge, education, and wisdom. But God's works cannot be accomplished through these things. For example, suppose there is a very good speaker who has the knowledge and speaking skills necessary to capture the audience. If that person delivers the message of God, can he make the believers change and live in the truth? The answer is that he absolutely cannot!

Of course, the audience may be touched by the speech for the moment. But that kind of speech has no power to move them to get rid of sinful natures or to remove the evil in their hearts. A person's knowledge and ability to speak well cannot lead them to live in the Word of God. Good speeches cannot plant faith in the hearts of the people. They cannot cause them to meet God or change their lives. Therefore the things that make such speeches are of no benefit.

If we understand this fact, we cannot help but become humble before God. We become weak, because we cannot do anything unless God is with us.

Even Jesus was weak at times, and He just avoided those people who were trying to capture and kill Him. The apostle Paul was also weak and he trembled before God, for he understood very well that he couldn't do anything if God was not with him.

Because the apostle Paul always had that fear and trembling, he never stopped praying in order to continue his spiritual communication with God. He was always on alert, not paying attention to anything else. In this same way we have to fulfill our God-given duties with weakness, fear, and trembling.

...and my message and my preaching were not in

persuasive words of wisdom, but in demonstration of
the Spirit and of power, so that your faith would not
rest on the wisdom of men, but on the power of God.
(2:4-5)

The Holy Spirit can begin to work only when we disregard
our worldly knowledge and wisdom. We have to rely on God
completely and entrust everything into His hands. Then, God
can control our hearts, minds, thoughts, and lips. If we pray for
wisdom in doing everything and not utilize human thoughts,
then we can hear the voice of the Holy Spirit coming from
within our heart. But if we use our own thoughts, we cannot
hear the voice of the Holy Spirit.

Some say they cannot hear the voice of the Holy Spirit even
though they pray. But it's not really true. Sometimes, they don't
just notice that they heard the voice of the Holy Spirit. Suppose
you want to begin something. Here, if you decide according to
your thoughts being unable to remember any Word of God,
then, you cannot hear the voice of the Holy Spirit. But if you
decide with the Word of God that is the truth and act according
to the truth, this is to hear the voice of the Holy Spirit.

God's Words do not come from our thoughts. Even though
they read the Bible extensively, those who do not receive the
power of the Holy Spirit are not able to remember the Word
of God under a variety of conditions and problem situations.
I believe some of you have experienced the following situation
a couple of times. You have read the Bible many times, but

when you want to give spiritual counsel to somebody, nothing appropriate seems to come to mind.

But to those who hear the voice of Holy Spirit will be given His Word so they can say what is needed for the people who need the spiritual counseling. Those who pray to God, those who arm themselves with the Word of God will hear the voice of the Holy Spirit all the time. It is in this way that by following the will of God they will always lead a life of victory and will not succumb to temptation by Satan.

Our faith cannot be gained through the wisdom of man. We cannot have faith and we cannot know God by human wisdom. It is often the contrary. The more wisdom one has the more doubt he is likely to have as well.

Because the apostle Paul understood this very clearly, he didn't use his wisdom, his ability to speak, and his personal knowledge. He was filled with the Holy Spirit, and being filled with the Spirit, He preached only Jesus Christ and the way of the cross. He put aside all his knowledge, and he did his ministry with the power of God and the Holy Spirit through prayers. That is how amazing healing works took place just by carrying handkerchiefs that had touched him to the sick (Acts 19:12).

The works of repentance will take place and people will change only when the message is preached by the power of God. When we show the power of God in the message preached, the knowledge of man and his thoughts will be shattered and the listener can acknowledge the living God. This is the way for them to gain faith, repent of their sins, and live in the truth. Therefore, when we preach the gospel, we have to testify to the living God by manifesting the power of God through prayers, not just with words or wisdom.

But this doesn't mean that we don't need any knowledge of the world and we don't have to study. What I have explained is that we shouldn't use worldly knowledge when we are accomplishing the works related to saving souls. We usually have to study hard in school and apply ourselves in our workplaces to edify others and give glory to God.

Whether we eat, drink, or whatever we do, we must live for the glory of God. It's the same with studying. It's just that we cannot plant faith in others just with our knowledge when we preach the gospel.

The Way of the Cross, the Wisdom of God

> Yet we do speak wisdom among those who are mature; a wisdom, however, not of this age nor of the rulers of this age, who are passing away; (2:6)

Up until now, the apostle Paul has explained that the wisdom of this world is useless. He said that he had set aside the wisdom of men, and he now talks about true wisdom. Here, 'those who are mature' means those who have grown up in faith, who stand on the rock of faith, and who eat solid food.

Let's take a closer look into wisdom a little more. James 3:17 says, *"But the wisdom from above is first pure, then peaceable, gentle, reasonable, full of mercy and good fruits, unwavering, without hypocrisy."*

This wisdom comes from above. It is given by God to the extent that we cast away what is not right according to the Word of God and live by His Word. Namely, if we live by the

Word, we will be pure, peaceable, gentle, reasonable, full of mercy and good fruits. We will be unwavering and without hypocrisy. We can receive wisdom from above to the extent that we accomplish the Word of God in us. Furthermore, we can receive limitless and endless wisdom from above if we go into the mature level of faith.

Those who reach this level of faith will not say that they cannot preach the gospel because they don't have enough education. They don't rely on their own knowledge but the wisdom from above. Concerning people who have attained this knowledge, in Matthew 10:19-20 it says, *"But when they hand you over, do not worry about how or what you are to say; for it will be given you in that hour what you are to say. For it is not you who speak, but it is the Spirit of your Father who speaks in you."*

To receive the wisdom from above, we have to give up worldly wisdom and knowledge. What specifically do we have to give up? Do we have to forget the knowledge such as, "One plus two is three"? Of course not!

We have to cast away the knowledge that is against the Word of God. Such an example is saying that monkeys have evolved to become human beings. We can understand such things are not true when we really understand the truth. We can believe God created the heavens and the earth and everything in them only after we get rid of such worldly knowledge.

Verse 6 says, "...a wisdom, however, not of this age nor of

the rulers of this age, who are passing away." Here, the rulers are civil workers. It refers to the Pharisees, the scribes, the priests, and those who were in the leadership positions.

As applied in today's use, the term 'rulers' refers to educators in leading positions, and those things through which we can be taught. Therefore, even teachers or books can be our rulers. When we didn't know the truth, we gained all kinds of knowledge and wisdom. But we have to discard much of it when we learn the truth.

For example, if you get sick, it is common knowledge and practice for people to go to the hospital and receive appropriate medical treatment. But those children of faith who believe in the almightiness of God can be healed completely through prayer. God's healing cannot be compared with any treatment of any hospital, for it will be perfect without leaving any after effects.

But the rulers of this world will not believe this fact; they would rather label it as foolishness. This is the wisdom of the rulers. With that wisdom, they cannot believe the truth.

...but we speak God's wisdom in a mystery, the hidden *wisdom* which God predestined before the ages to our glory; (2:7)

God created the heavens and earth to gain true children and made all the provisions for the human cultivation. God knew when Adam would disobey and go the way of death.

Knowing this, God hid the providence of salvation that was to come through Jesus Christ. That is why Jesus Christ is the secret hidden since before time began.

When Jesus Christ appeared to people, the rulers of this age didn't understand Him with their wisdom. They crucified Jesus. The enemy devil brings to people only worldly wisdom and knowledge. The devil didn't understand God's wisdom, and he thought he would be able to have the ruling authority of the air forever, but only if he killed Jesus.

From the time of Jesus' birth the enemy the devil tried every way possible to kill Jesus. Finally, he incited the rulers of this age to crucify Jesus, and he thought he was victorious. But this was in the wisdom of God.

A spiritual law dictates that the wages of sin is death. Before he ate the forbidden fruit, Adam was sinless and there was no death. Only after his disobedience did Adam and his descendants come to face death. If one commits sins, he will surely face death. But the devil killed the sinless Jesus who didn't have either original sin or sins that He had committed. Thus, when the devil incited people to kill Jesus, it was in violation of the law of the spiritual realm.

Originally, Adam had the authority to rule over and subdue all things on earth. But when he sinned, his authority was handed over to the devil because Adam obeyed him by committing a sin. But as a consequence of the devil killing sinless Jesus, the devil had to return his authority over the nations. From that moment on, anyone who believes in Jesus Christ can be saved. This is the 'way of cross' that was hidden since before time began. It was God's plan to save the sinners. How amazing God's wisdom is!

God gives us wisdom from above when we cast off the wisdom of the devil which is the wisdom and knowledge of the rulers of this age. If we receive God's wisdom from above, we can enjoy limitless glory on earth.

Then, why does it say that we will receive glory while only God is supposed to receive all the glory? We give glory to God the Father in all things, whether we eat, drink, or whatever we do. Then, He gives back to us pressed down, shaken together, and running over after He receives the glory because He loves giving.

He also gives us rewards in Heaven. Thus, if we give glory to God, it is, after all, giving glory to ourselves, too. God leads us to salvation, and to eternal life from death, and thus, this is to our glory.

Jesus also always gave glory to God the Father. But John 17:10 says, *"I have been glorified in them."* Because Jesus received the reward of sitting on the right hand of God's throne and the authority to rule over all nations, He is glorified.

the wisdom **which none of the rulers of this age has understood; for if they had understood it they would**

not have crucified the Lord of glory; but just as it is written, "Things which eye has not seen and ear has not heard, and which have not entered the heart of man, all that God has prepared for those who love Him." (2:8-9)

Some rulers of this age also believed in God, but it says, "the wisdom which none of the rulers of this age has understood." This means if we teach and utilize the worldly wisdom, we cannot understand Jesus Christ. If they had known the wisdom of God, they wouldn't have crucified Jesus.

Those teachers do not give up on their worldly wisdom and that is why they cannot receive wisdom from above. That is why they didn't know Jesus Christ, the secret hidden since before time began, but instead they crucified Him.

Verse 9 says, "Things which eye has not seen and ear has not heard, and which have not entered the heart of man, all that God has prepared for those who love Him." Those who teach the knowledge of this world that is contrary to the Word of God and who do not practice the Word of God cannot see or hear even though they have eyes and ears. They cannot hear the voice of the Holy Spirit, and they persecute those who preach the Word of truth to them. The result is that in the end, they crucify Jesus.

Then, why is it that they cannot see, hear, or think? It's because they become spiritually blinded because of their worldly knowledge that is against the truth. Therefore, the apostle Paul advised them to cast away the worldly knowledge that was against the Word of truth and receive the wisdom from God in order to lead a blessed life.

God's Grace Understood through the Holy Spirit

For to us God revealed *them* through the Spirit; for the Spirit searches all things, even the depths of God. (2:10)

We can neither meet nor understand God with the knowledge and wisdom of this world. But if we open our hearts and accept Jesus Christ, we will receive the gift of the Holy Spirit and then we can come to know and meet God. The Holy Spirit is the spirit of God, namely the heart of God. Then, how can the Holy Spirit lead us to know and meet God?

The Holy Spirit teaches us that God is the Creator and our Father. He lets us know the secret that was hidden since before time began. It is the secret that the rulers of this age do not understand. He teaches us about Jesus Christ and leads us to have faith by teaching us about Heaven and Hell. The Holy Spirit is the heart of the holy God and it is natural that He is able to search even the deep things of God.

When the Holy Spirit comes to us, He revives our dead spirit and leads us to the truth. Furthermore, He allows for us to confess that Jesus is our Lord. He also testifies that we belong to God.

Additionally, the Holy Spirit teaches us and reminds us of all things Jesus taught us. As John 14:26 says, *"But the Helper, the Holy Spirit, whom the Father will send in My name, He will teach you all things, and bring to your remembrance all that I said to you."* He also helps us with our weaknesses and makes it possible for us to pray according to the will of God.

The Holy Spirit knows the heart of God completely and He wants the will of God to be fulfilled. So, He helps God's children to pray according to God's will. Moreover, as said in Galatians 5:22-23, *"But the fruit of the Spirit is love, joy, peace, patience, kindness, goodness, faithfulness, gentleness, self-control; against such things there is no law,"* through Him we can bear the fruit of the Spirit. He guides us to become spiritual persons who practice the will of God.

For who among men knows the *thoughts* of a man except the spirit of the man which is in him? Even so the *thoughts* of God no one knows except the Spirit of God. (2:11)

The apostle Paul mentions the spirit of men to explain about the Holy Spirit. Nobody knows the thoughts of a man except the spirit of the man which is in him. Likewise, the Holy Spirit knows the deep things of God. When this Holy Spirit comes to us, we will also know the things of God, and thus, we will also receive the wisdom of God and understand the deep things of God.

But here, Paul could have said it was the heart or conscience of a man that knows the thoughts of the man, but why did he say it was the spirit of the man which is in him? Here lies a deep spiritual meaning.

When we accept Jesus Christ and receive the gift of the Holy Spirit and live as God's children, our heart is 'spirit' itself. But we should understand and distinguish that there is heart and there is spirit in a man.

In Genesis, after He created the first man Adam, God said to him, *"From any tree of the garden you may eat freely; but from the tree of the knowledge of good and evil you shall not eat, for in the day that you eat from it you will surely die"* (Genesis 2:17). Then the LORD God said, *"It is not good for the man to be alone; I will make him a helper suitable for him"* (v.18), and took a rib from Adam and from it He gave him a woman to become one flesh.

God set Adam to rule over everything and blessed the man when He said, *"Be fruitful and multiply, and fill the earth, and subdue it; and rule over the fish of the sea and over the birds of the sky and over every living thing that moves on the earth"* (Genesis 1:28).

One day, Satan tempted Eve through the serpent, *"Indeed, has God said, 'You shall not eat from any tree of the garden'?"* (Genesis 3:1)

Eve answered, *"From the fruit of the trees of the garden we may eat; but from the fruit of the tree which is in the middle of the garden, God has said, 'You shall not eat from it or touch it, or you will die'"* (v.3). God said, "You will surely die," but Eve said, "You will die," being less certain.

Then, the Satan more progressively tempted Eve saying, *"You surely will not die! For God knows that in the day you eat from it your eyes will be opened, and you will be like God, knowing good and evil"* (v.3-4). Eve finally ate the fruit and gave it to Adam, and he ate it too. They were deceived and disobeyed God because they didn't keep His Word.

As God had spoken, *"You will surely die,"* when Adam ate the forbidden fruit in the Garden of Eden, his spirit died. From that time on he could no longer communicate with God. But John 3:6 says, *"That which is born of the flesh is flesh, and that which is born of the Spirit is spirit."* As said, when we accept the Lord, the Holy Spirit comes into us and gives life to our spirit. Namely, He lets us realize what sin is, what righteousness is, and what judgment is. He teaches us the Word of God, so our dead spirit is revived and we become more of a spiritual person. This is referred to as 'the Spirit giving birth to spirit.'

Therefore, without the Holy Spirit, our dead spirit cannot be revived nor can we give birth to our spirit. We can understand the Word of the truth, take it as our spiritual bread, and live a life of a man of spirit to become a completely spiritual person. This is done only through the Holy Spirit. We accomplish the image of the Lord through this process.

The prophets and the disciples of Jesus all became men of spirit this way and communicated with God so that they could manifest powerful works of God in accomplishing His kingdom. John 14:12 says, *"Truly, truly, I say to you, he who believes in Me, the works that I do, he will do also; and greater works than these he will do; because I go to the Father."* If we become men of spirit, we will be able to manifest signs and wonders and do even greater things than these for the glory of God.

Before Adam ate from the tree of the knowledge of good and evil, there was no need to distinguish between heart and spirit. His spirit was his heart itself. But since he sinned and his spirit died, untruths came into men's hearts. It is from this point that man's heart was divided into the heart of truth and the heart of untruth. We have these two kinds of heart. One part wants to follow the desire of the Holy Spirit and the other part wants to follow the desires of the flesh.

In other words, we have the desire to seek the truth, goodness, and spirit, and another desire to seek untruth, evilness, and flesh. The more spiritual we become, the more we can control the desires of the flesh and follow the desires of the

Holy Spirit. If we control the desires of the flesh completely, we won't feel leading a life in Christ is difficult, but only have joy and happiness in it.

But if we have a stronger desire to follow the flesh, we are likely to lose in our spiritual battles. If our hearts are divided exactly into two halves being one half that is the heart of truth and the other, the heart of untruth, then leading a life in Christ is difficult because there are always intense struggles. But if we have the stronger desire to follow the Holy Spirit, then we will always tend toward leading a life of victory. If we continually 'give birth to spirit' through the Spirit this way, we will be able to get rid of the untruthful things in the heart and our hearts be filled completely with the truth. Then, our spirit and heart are one.

Only the spirit in the man knows all thoughts of a man. You may think you know your heart very well, but it's not true. For example, many people make New Year's resolutions. Some of them make up their mind to live in the Word of God and others intend to try harder to expand their businesses.

Some students may decide to study harder and get good grades. If these people keep their resolutions for just half of the year, it is something excellent and extraordinary. It means they don't even know their heart. Suppose you are praying to God for financial problems. You may say, "God, if You bless me financially, I will help the needy and spend it for Your glory! You know my heart and please bless me!" But in many cases they don't receive an answer to their prayers.

God wants to give to His children when they ask, so why doesn't He? It's because He knows their heart.

They may think that they will help the poor since they also suffered from poverty, but only God knows their inner heart. God cannot bless them if He thinks, "No, if I give you financial blessings, you will distance yourself from Me. You will love money more than Me, you will not pray, and you will gradually fall into the world."

In fact, there are quite a few people who stop praying and fall into the world once they receive financial blessings. When they are in need, they work faithfully for the kingdom of God, but once they receive blessings, they distance themselves from God. They give excuses that they are busy or have no time. In these cases, you see that they are more blessed not to receive financial blessings so that they will not leave God.

It is in this way that we don't know our own hearts, but the spirit in us does. Those who arm themselves with the Word of God and completely live in the truth know their hearts. They know whether or not they have cunningness or whether they will be able to keep their promises. Their spirit lets them know these things, and they will not make a mistake before God.

For example, they won't just pray, "God, I will do it!" They will say something like, "God, I want to do it, so give me Your strength and help me!" God tells us not to vow by anything

(Matthew 5:34). If we make a vow, Satan may try to disturb us so we will not be able to keep it. That is why we pray, "God, help me and give me the strength to do it."

But if your spirit acknowledges that you can surely do something, you will be able to say in your prayer, "God, I will do it, please help me," and you will surely get it done. Because you made a promise before God and with yourself, you will certainly do it. The spirit of the truth in us knows our inner thoughts, and it can pray precisely according to our situation.

But if we are not men of spirit yet, we are not able to really hear the voice of the Holy Spirit. We can only check ourselves with our heart, and we cannot really understand the deep things. This is the reason why we cannot really anticipate tomorrow.

There is one thing we should remember. It is written, "For who among men knows the thoughts of a man except the spirit of the man which is in him?" If you become a man of truth, you will be able to avoid even dangerous things, because the Holy Spirit will let you know about it through a dream, inspiration, or voice in heart, or during your prayers. The Holy Spirit searches even the deep things of God, and He will let us know. To the extent that we become men of spirit, we will hear those voices of the Holy Spirit more clearly.

Therefore, if you clearly understand the spiritual Word of God and realize the truth, it is something very natural for you to communicate with God. You will be able to act appropriately in all things if you become men of spirit. The Holy Spirit is in us, and if we listen to His voice, we can understand God's heart and will and please Him.

Now we have received, not the spirit of the world, but the Spirit who is from God, so that we may know the things freely given to us by God. (2:12)

Those who have accepted Jesus Christ and received the Holy Spirit have received the gift of the Spirit of God, not the spirit of this world. Then, what is the spirit of the world? It is the spirit of the devil, the deceiving spirit, and the spirit of falsehood.

Even among believers in God we can find some who have received the spirit of deception and falsehood. For example, they are people who say they cannot believe the signs and wonders recorded in the Bible.

The Bible records occurrences of many signs and wonders. These take place because God creates things from nothing. Thus, it is not right to disbelieve God with one's own thoughts and theories. These people may say they believe, but they haven't really given birth to spirit through the Spirit. They are not children of God.

What does the Bible say about the spirit of the world?

1 Timothy 4:1 says, *"But the Spirit explicitly says that in later times some will fall away from the faith, paying attention to deceitful spirits and doctrines of demons."* We will not be deceived if we stand firm on the rock of faith. Those who forsake their faith will follow the deceitful spirits and doctrines of demons.

For example, when the Bible tells us to cry out in prayer, we should obviously obey it in our praying. But some people try to stop others from crying out in prayer saying that God is not deaf. Also, God's Word tells us to try to gather together all the time, but some don't want to gather saying they are busy. These things are the teachings of the deceitful spirits.

1 John 4:3 says, *"Every spirit that does not confess Jesus is not from God; this is the spirit of the antichrist, of which you have heard that it is coming, and now it is already in the world."* Verse 6 says, *"He who is not from God does not listen to us. By this we know the spirit of truth and the spirit of error."*

In Revelation 16:13 it is written, *"And I saw coming out of the mouth of the dragon and out of the mouth of the beast and out of the mouth of the false prophet, three unclean spirits like frogs."* It talks about the unclean spirits. Revelation 16:14 continues, *"For they are spirits of demons, performing signs, which go out to the kings of the whole world, to gather them together for the war of the great day of God, the Almighty."* It talks about the spirits of demons.

Revelation 18:2 says, *"And he cried out with a mighty voice, saying, 'Fallen, fallen is Babylon the great! She has become a dwelling place of demons and a prison of every unclean spirit, and a prison of every unclean and hateful bird.'"*

If one receives a spirit of the world like the above, he will depart from the truth and follow the world. To him following the Word of God seems rather strange. To him it becomes something completely normal since he is receiving the works of demons and deceitful spirits.

But true children of God do not receive the spirit of the world but only the Spirit of God, the Holy Spirit. 1 Corinthians 2:12 explains the reason of giving us the Holy Spirit. It says, *"Now we have received, not the spirit of the world, but the Spirit who is from God, so that we may know the things freely given to us by God."*

If we are paid for our work, it is not grace. We are just paid for what we have done. But if we receive something without doing any work, it is grace.

We are not saved because we did something or because we lived a righteous life. Matthew 9:13 says, *"I did not come to call the righteous, but sinners."* Jesus came to call the sinners. We can now cast away sins and live a righteous life because Jesus called us who were sinners. We are forgiven of sins through Jesus Christ and we can overcome the world by the strength of God.

Spiritual Things Are Discerned through the Spirit

These things we also speak, not in words which man's wisdom teaches but which the Holy Spirit teaches, comparing spiritual things with spiritual. (2:13, NKJV)

The apostle Paul did not preach the gospel with the wisdom of word or men's teaching. He did not refer to any books or other studies but taught only what the Holy Spirit taught him.

There are many people who have much wisdom and knowledge of the world. But having increased knowledge of the world does not enable a person to do the work of God better. For example, even a CEO of a big company may not be able to perform a small duty in the church.

That is why 1 Corinthians 2:4 says, *"My message and my preaching were not with wise and persuasive words, but with a demonstration of the Spirit's power."* God's works cannot be achieved by human knowledge or wisdom. They have to be done only with a demonstration of the Spirit's power.

It's the same with the revival of churches. Some famous people who were formerly presidents or professors of universities and leaders in the society have become pastors.

We may think they ought to be able to bring about a great revival in the church because they have so much knowledge and wisdom. But it doesn't really happen that way. God's works cannot be achieved by wisdom and knowledge of men. We have to do God's works only according to the teaching of the Holy Spirit. What does He teach? Let us find out in the Bible how He works to revive the dead spirit and leads the revived spirit to the truth.

John 14:26 says, *"But the Counselor, the Holy Spirit, whom the Father will send in my name, will teach you all things and will remind you of everything I have said to you."* We have to receive this teaching and guidance of the Holy Spirit.

Luke 12:11-12 says, *"When they bring you before the synagogues and the rulers and the authorities, do not worry about how or what you are to speak in your defense, or what you are to say; for the Holy Spirit will teach you in that very hour what you ought to say."* Thus, there won't be any mistake if we hear Holy Spirit's voice and follow His guidance.

In whatever we do, if the Holy Spirit doesn't work, we will only have human thoughts, and thus we cannot experience the power of God. Therefore, we have to work through the manifestation of the Spirit's power, not with man's wisdom or knowledge.

Things of the Flesh and Works of the Flesh

Verse 13 concludes with the words, "...comparing spiritual things with spiritual" (NKJV). What are spiritual things? If there are spiritual things, there must be things that are not spiritual. Let us first look at the things that are not spiritual. They refer to the things of the flesh and the works of the flesh.

Things of the flesh refer to the sinful attributes that can be triggered to become actions of sin, such as envy, jealousy, or hatred.

The 'flesh' in the Bible is the generic term for 'sinful actions and sinful natures.' The 'works of the flesh' refer to the resulting actions of sin. If we have a desire to hit somebody, it is a 'thing of the flesh,' and if we actually hit that person, it is a 'work of the flesh.'

Romans 13:14 says, *"But put on the Lord Jesus Christ, and make no provision for the flesh in regard to its lusts."* Galatians 5:19-21 talks about the works of the flesh that are opposite of spiritual things. It says, *"Now the works of the flesh are evident, which are: adultery, fornication, uncleanness, lewdness, idolatry, sorcery, hatred, contentions, jealousies, outbursts of wrath, selfish ambitions, dissensions, heresies, envy, murders, drunkenness, revelries, and the like; of which I tell you beforehand, just as I also told you in time past, that those who practice such things will not inherit the kingdom of God"* (NKJV).

These works of the flesh are harmful to ourselves and they also cause pain to others. They prevent us from inheriting the kingdom of God and receiving answers from God.

Thus, 'spiritual things' means departing from or getting rid of the things of the flesh and the works of the flesh. Once we get into this level, we will have communication with God, receive answers to whatever we ask, and glorify Him.

God's children are in the process of becoming men of spirit, and most believers are not really complete men of spirit who can be acknowledged by God. Each individual has a different measure of faith, and we can discern the spiritual things properly only when we enter into the spiritual levels.

But a natural man does not accept the things of the Spirit of God, for they are foolishness to him; and he cannot understand them, because they are spiritually appraised. (2:14)

Here, 'a natural man' refers to a person who does not keep the Word of God and has not come into the truth yet, namely he who loves the world and still has worldly desires in him.

Such people cannot hear the voice of the Holy Spirit and they cannot be guided by Him. The Holy Spirit always teaches us and guides us, but if the spiritual ears are closed to hearing

His voice, spiritual things cannot be discerned. The natural man thinks spiritual men are rather awkwardly dull.

Even if we may not receive blessings in our business or in workplace, to live in the Word of God is a blessing. Worldly people tend to say if one is wealthy he is blessed, but the Bible does not say God's blessing is only about financial blessing.

Psalm 1:1-2 says, *"How blessed is the man who does not walk in the counsel of the wicked, nor stand in the path of sinners, nor sit in the seat of scoffers! But his delight is in the law of the LORD, and in His law he meditates day and night."*

As we can learn from the parable of the rich man and Lazarus the beggar, wealth on this earth is not true blessing. Lazarus was blessed, for he served God and received salvation. This earthly life is only for a brief moment, but the heavenly kingdom is eternal. Those who can accept this word with joy can go into the spiritual level.

Only those who receive the works of the Spirit of God can understand this. This way, they can abstain from falling into the works of the flesh and live in the truth. As said in the passage, 1 Corinthians 2:14, we can compare [discern] such things only by the spirit.

To 'compare' means to discern between two things. The truth tells us which is right, but those who have the works of the flesh are not able to consider the two things properly. They think their own idea must be correct. But they can discern what is really correct only when they get into the spiritual dimension.

But he who is spiritual appraises all things, yet he himself is appraised by no one. (2:15)

Many parts of the Bible tell us not to judge others. So what does this verse mean? 'He who is spiritual' is somebody who is living in the Word of truth. Because he is living in the Word of the truth of God completely, he understands the meaning in it, and can appraise anybody.

Here, what does this 'appraise' mean? A spiritual man would not hate or become envious of anybody, nor would he become arrogant to pass judgment on others. His appraisal would be appraisal of love.

Matthew 7:3-5 says, *"Why do you look at the speck that is in your brother's eye, but do not notice the log that is in your own eye? Or how can you say to your brother, 'Let me take the speck out of your eye,' and behold, the log is in your own eye? You hypocrite, first take the log out of your own eye, and then you will see clearly to take the speck out of your brother's eye."*

It tells us that if we take 'the log' out of our eyes, we can clearly see others. To take the log out of our eyes means to cast away all fleshly things from us. Those who live in the truth naturally love God and their brothers. They don't have any envy, jealousy, or arrogance. They look at the brothers only with love, and only those people can clearly see the speck of their brothers. 'He who is spiritual' in the passage refers to this kind of man of spirit.

Then, who can judge a man of spirit?

The worldly people easily pass judgment on others. They don't know what spiritual things are, and they just think they are right. So, they consider spiritual people to be foolish and pass judgment on them. The Pharisees, the scribes, and unbelievers passed judgment and condemnation on Jesus. But in fact, those who do not know spiritual things cannot judge those who are spiritual.

It's like an elementary school student cannot judge the mathematical skills of a college student. Only when the child goes to the college and surpasses the point in education of the college student can he judge whether or not this college student is good at math. Thus, spiritual men can appraise anybody, but those who are not spiritual cannot appraise spiritual men.

For who has known the mind of the Lord, that he will instruct Him? But we have the mind of Christ. (2:16)

Can you teach somebody who is more spiritual than you? I am asking whether or not you can teach somebody who hears the voice of the Holy Spirit better than you. If you do, it means you are trying to teach God Himself. If you try to teach a man who hears the voice of the Holy Spirit clearly, then it implies that you place yourself higher than God.

Therefore, we have to strictly keep the order of the church.

Satan begins to work if the order is broken. That is why Paul said, "For who has known the mind of the Lord, that he will instruct Him?" Upon hearing it, the believers may be discouraged, and that is why he said, *"But we have the mind of Christ"* in verse 16. We shouldn't be disappointed, because we have the mind of the Christ.

The Holy Spirit dwells in us. Thus, if we live in the truth, we can hear His voice to resemble the Lord and become more spiritual, being enabled to compare and discern spiritual things. Then, we can be considered as true sons of God.

Romans 8:14 says, *"For all who are being led by the Spirit of God, these are sons of God."* It's not just anybody but those who are being led by the Spirit of God; they are the sons of God. Therefore, let us enter into the spiritual dimensions and become sons of God who are led by the Spirit of God.

Chapter 3

WE ARE GOD'S TEMPLE

— The Corinthian Church Belonged to the Flesh

— God Causes the Growth

— A Wise Master Builder

— Each One's Work

— Destroying the Temple of God

— Worldly Wisdom is Foolish

The Corinthian Church Belonged to the Flesh

And I, brethren, could not speak to you as to spiritual men, but as to men of flesh, as to infants in Christ. (3:1)

Paul says, "I could not speak to you as to spiritual men..." From this, we can see the believers of the Corinthian church had not yet become people of the spirit. Paul could not speak to them as to spiritual men and women because they were still people of the flesh. They were people who befriended the world and belonged to flesh.

Paul has this to say to describe such people who have not yet attained a level of spirit, "...but as to men of flesh, as to infants in Christ." Infants cannot digest solid food. If they were to eat solid food while not being able to digest it, the food would put their lives at risk. That is why we have to feed infants on milk.

Likewise, those who say they believe in God, but still dwell in flesh, cannot take in and understand the Word of God. They cannot live by His Word. Even though they may be acknowledged as intellectuals in this world, they are still infants in Christ who do not know the truth.

> I gave you milk to drink, not solid food; for you were not yet able *to receive* it. Indeed, even now you are not yet able, (3:2)

The apostle Paul said he did not give them solid food, but milk to drink. As explained in verse 1, the believers in the church of Corinth were spiritual infants who could not digest solid food. That is why Paul said he had to give them only milk, for they could not handle spiritual things.

We can understand that the believers in the Corinthian church were still fleshly people from chapter 1 of 1 Corinthians as well. They had factions within the church who said, "'I am of Paul', 'I am of Apollos', and 'I am of Cephas.'" This means that they were not united as one in the truth.

Had they known how to eat spiritual food, they would have united as one in love to pray, follow the will of God, and save more souls. But because they were still spiritual infants who had to drink milk, they insisted that they were right. It means they were not partaking of spiritual things.

What kind of faith do we have to have in order to become steadfast spiritual men and women of faith?

If we think of spiritual faith measured as percentiles, then spiritual men and women are those who have passed through the 60th percentile of the third level of faith. At 50th percentile they may be swayed to the left or to the right. But at 60th they won't be shaken and they are able to overcome the desires of the flesh. Thus, we can say they 'stand on the rock of faith'. From this stage on they can be called spiritual men and women and they will seek after spiritual things.

Please, will you check yourself to see where you are on a scale of one to one hundred right now? If you are at 10th or 20th percentiles of faith, it means you are still spiritually infants. As explained previously, even though they are adults in this world, they can spiritually be infants if they cannot take in and comprehend solid, spiritual things. If such is the case, then they have to hear the Word and practice it diligently to become mature believers.

Also, spiritually, new-believers are like spiritual infants. According to their measure of faith we have to spiritually nurture and care for them. Suppose a new-believer is running a shop. On Sundays, because he is still at the level of a spiritual infant, he may attend the worship service in the morning and later open his shop. If he closes his shop on Sundays, God will bless him. But he doesn't have the faith to accept the truth of it yet.

If we tell such a person that, to keep the Lord's Day holy,

he has to close the shop completely on Sunday and spend the whole day at the church, he will feel very much burdened and just refuse to do it.

Therefore, we have to teach them step by step how to keep the Lord's Day holy. We could offer a suggestion saying, "If you don't want to close the shop on Sundays, you could still open the shop, but pray to God to increase your faith. And as your faith increases you will be willing to close the shop and attend church." Because they are at the state of loving money more than God now, we should not give them spiritual indigestion!

If his faith grows up and if he can spiritually start eating soft food, he may normally close the shop on Sunday, but on major holidays he might not overcome the temptation and open the shop. He cannot keep the Lord's Day holy with joy. This is the stage where he spiritually eats soft food. Up to this stage, we say that they 'belong to flesh'.

But if one becomes a spiritual man, he will close the shop on Sundays and keep the Lord's Day holy even though it might mean he will face some financial loss. A believer who is a spiritual person is unwilling to exchange the kingdom of Heaven for a little more money, and will not disobey God's Word for personal gain. Also, spiritual men rejoice to do it because they know that it is not financial loss to close the shop on Sundays. They please God by keeping the Word with faith and rejoice in the fact that they are recognized as God's children. We say these people are 'standing on the rock of faith'.

for you are still fleshly. For since there is jealousy and strife among you, are you not fleshly, and are you not walking like mere men? (3:3)

The apostle Paul was emphasizing that the believers in the Corinthian church were still fleshly by pointing out that there was still jealousy and strife among them.

To be jealous is to be hostile toward a rival or one believed to enjoy an advantage. Strife is bitter, or sometimes violent conflict or dissension. It starts from greed, and it causes quarrels.

As explained already, the members of the Corinthian church were saying they were of Paul, Cephas, Apollos, or the Christ to cause jealousy and strife. Not only at that time, but there are still churches that have strife and dissensions in the church today.

For example, members of a missionary group in a church have to obey the leader of the group. Let's say that the leader is selected by demonstrating attributes that are more spiritually advanced than others. If members of the group don't obey the leader, there is jealousy and strife involved.

Suppose you have some discomfort about your leader thinking, "I learned more than he did, and I have greater faith than he does!" Then, what would God think of you? God cannot but say you are fleshly, just like in the case of the members of the Corinthian church. Therefore, if we have such mind, we have to quickly cast it away and become spiritual men and women.

For when one says, 'I am of Paul,' and another, 'I am of Apollos,' are you not mere men? What then is Apollos? And what is Paul? Servants through whom you believed, even as the Lord gave *opportunity* to each one (3:4-5)

Acts 4:12 says, *"And there is salvation in no one else; for there is no other name under heaven that has been given among men by which we must be saved."* As recorded, we receive salvation by the name of Jesus Christ. The apostle Paul, Apollos, or somebody else may have great power, but it doesn't mean we can be saved through them.

But when the believers in the church of Corinth said they were of 'this person' or 'that person', Paul said Apollos and he were ministers. Ministers are those who have received a duty from somebody and fulfill it. The apostle Paul and Apollos were ministers of God and servants of God who were doing the work of saving souls.

Ministers do not act upon their will but the will of God. Therefore, Apollos or Paul obeyed the will of God to save the souls by planting faith in the flock and carefully tended to them. Salvation comes from the Christ alone, and so, Paul was very concerned about the believers in Corinth because they said that they were 'of Paul' or 'of Apollos'.

God Causes the Growth

I planted, Apollos watered, but God was causing the growth. (3:6)

Apollos accepted the Lord earlier than the apostle Paul, but God considered the vessel of the apostle Paul and made him greater than Apollos in manifesting the power of God. They were all one in God, but Paul planted and Apollos watered.

"Paul planted" means that he planted the seed of faith in the hearts of people. He testified to the living God with signs, and people gained faith. This way the seed of faith was planted in them.

Jesus also planted faith through signs and wonders. If He had not manifested any signs and wonders, then, nobody would have believed Him to be the Son of God, the Savior.

There are many signs and wonders Jesus performed that are recorded in the Bible. In Mark 4 we find He calmed down the wind and waves. Matthew 4:23-24 says, *"Jesus was going throughout all Galilee, teaching in their synagogues and proclaiming the gospel of the kingdom, and healing every kind of disease and every kind of sickness among the people. The news about Him spread throughout all Syria; and they brought to Him all who were ill, those suffering with various diseases and pains, demoniacs, epileptics, paralytics; and He healed them."*

In the same way, Jesus' disciples and the apostle Paul planted faith through the signs they manifested. That is how so many people could believe and accept the gospel.

Apollos watered. Once a seed is planted, it has to be watered. Here, the water spiritually means the Word of God. Pastors and leaders have to give the Word of God to the believers so their faith can grow up. In this way, all work together to accomplish the kingdom of God.

Of course, by saying that the apostle Paul planted faith and Apollos helped the faith to grow, it doesn't mean planting and watering are separate. The one who waters can also plant faith and the one who plants faith can also water. Both the apostle Paul and Apollos planted and watered, but it's just that the apostle Paul mainly planted and Apollos watered.

So then neither the one who plants nor the one who waters is anything, but God who causes the growth. (3:7)

After the seed is sown and it is watered, it is useless unless it grows up by the power of God. It is by the power of God that a seed that is planted sprouts and grows up.

In spirit as well, God through His ministers plants faith and waters the people to obey His Word and lead a blessed life. But neither the one who plants nor the one who waters is anything.

It is only God who causes the growth. The Apostle Paul planted and Apollos watered, but it was still useless unless God caused the growth. Thus, both the one who plants and the one who waters have to give all the glory to God.

Now he who plants and he who waters are one; but each will receive his own reward according to his own labor. (3:8)

He who plants and he who waters are one because they are all workers of God. If the seed is not planted properly, watering it will be useless. Only when ministers work together and plant and water properly, can everything be done through grace.

That is why it says, "Now he who plants and he who waters are one; but each will receive his own reward according to his own labor." Each one has a different vessel. Some show signs, some others preach, and still others give spiritual care for the believers, praise God, or do voluntary works. Each one will receive his own reward according to his deeds.

Not all pastors will just receive greater rewards. The rewards are given according to how well each one sanctifies himself and fulfills his duty. They don't depend on the title itself.

Students may think, "I am a student, and the only thing I do is to study, so how can I have any reward in the kingdom of Heaven?" The thinking is unfounded. God gave the students a duty, too. It is to pray and worship God and study well as students to give glory to God. Also, if they give out the fragrance of Christ wherever they are and earn the praise of others by respecting their parents, such things will become their rewards.

Since children also have their duties, they also have rewards in the kingdom of Heaven. Their duties are to attend worship service without crying, to pray and not to cause trouble. For this reason, the rewards of the children will be different according to how their parents raise them in faith.

Even pastors may face stricter judgment if they do not fulfill their duty of taking care of the souls entrusted to them. That is why James 3:1 says, *"Let not many of you become teachers, my brethren, knowing that as such we will incur a stricter judgment."*

For we are God's fellow workers; you are God's field, God's building. (3:9)

Fellow workers are those who work together to accomplish the same work. The apostle Paul and Apollos were fellow workers for they worked together for the salvation of souls planting and watering, and accomplishing the kingdom of God.

Paul said, "You are God's field." The field referred to is the heart of men. The heart of those who have faith is the field of God, and that is why we have to take care of it very well.

In Matthew 13, 'field' is categorized into good soil, thorny field, rocky field, and soil along the path. God's children have to make their heart the good soil.

Paul also said, "You are the house of God." Those children of God who have received the Holy Spirit are a house of God because the Holy Spirit dwells in them.

That's why in 1 Corinthians 3:16-17 it says, *"Do you not know that you are a temple of God and that the Spirit of God dwells in you? If any man destroys the temple of God, God will destroy him, for the temple of God is holy, and that is what you are."*

We are the field of God and God's dwelling place, as such we should be spiritual men, not fleshly men who have jealousy and act in untruth.

A Wise Master Builder

According to the grace of God which was given to me, like a wise master builder I laid a foundation, and another is building on it. But each man must be careful how he builds on it. (3:10)

This verse seems easy to understand in its literal meaning. But there are three important spiritual meanings. This kind of verse is like the word in a cord of three strands.

The literal interpretation of the verse 10 is the first cord. This only applies to the apostle Paul. There are two other strands that apply to us. Combining the part that applies to Paul and the parts that apply to us, it becomes the three-strand cord.

'Me' here refers to the apostle Paul. His name before he met the Lord was Saul. He was a strict Jew and severely persecuted those who believed in Jesus.

He received an official document from the priest to arrest

those who believed in Jesus Christ and bring them to Jerusalem. On his way to Damascus, he met Jesus Christ. In Acts chapter 9, it explains in detail how Saul accepted the Lord.

From the time that Saul met the Lord on the way to Damascus, he came to love Him deeply. Romans 8:35-39 says, *"Who will separate us from the love of Christ? Will tribulation, or distress, or persecution, or famine, or nakedness, or peril, or sword? Just as it is written, 'For Your sake we are being put to death all day long; We were considered as sheep to be slaughtered.' But in all these things we overwhelmingly conquer through Him who loved us. For I am convinced that neither death, nor life, nor angels, nor principalities, nor things present, nor things to come, nor powers, nor height, nor depth, nor any other created thing, will be able to separate us from the love of God, which is in Christ Jesus our Lord."*

The apostle Paul knew that the knowledge of Jesus Christ was the most precious. Comparatively he counted all other things to be only loss and rubbish. He became a passionate preacher of the gospel as he went wherever God wanted him to go.

He prayed according to the will of God. And in Acts 19:12 we find that when handkerchiefs or aprons that had just touched his body were carried to the sick, diseases left them and the evil spirits went out from them.

The apostle Paul was commissioned as a missionary from the church in Antioch and established churches in many places. He preached the gospel in Corinth, Galatia, and many other places and opened many new churches.

He put either a servant of God or a worker of God in charge of each church to pastor the church, and then left that place to further spread the gospel. At this time, he said to those who were in charge of the churches, "According to the grace of God which was given to me, like a wise master builder, I laid a foundation and another is building on it. But each man must be careful how he builds on it."

Paul was like a wise master builder. He professed and testified to Jesus Christ according to the grace of God and laid the foundation. It is here that he is now urging pastors in the churches to testify to the gospel of Jesus Christ just like he did.

This is the first strand of the cord that tells us the situation of the apostle Paul at the time in relation to the church. The second and the third strand of the cord that tell us the will of God today are even more significant and important today.

What is the second meaning given by God in this verse?

It is that we, the children of God, have to build upon and continue building the sanctuary of the heart with care and diligence. When we open our heart and accept Jesus Christ, the Holy Spirit comes into our hearts. We now become a temple of God because the Holy Spirit is in our heart (1 Corinthians 3:16).

Then, how are we supposed to build the temple of God? In the beginning, that is the time before we received the Holy Spirit, we were a building being built upon by the devil. We were not a temple of God. Some may wonder why I say this, but let's think for a moment about what kind of people we were before receiving the Holy Spirit.

Our mind was incited by Satan and we committed the deeds of the devil. We enjoyed seeing and hearing many different kinds of unclean things, we went to unclean places, and we liked committing unclean acts. We enjoyed doing what was not according to the truth, and thus, we were a building that was built upon by the devil.

Then, as God tells us to be holy, by the help of the Holy Spirit, we began the struggle against sins. Our heart changes with the truth. We come to think in truth, and our will and plans come from the truth. This way, we destroy the building of the devil and build up the temple of God.

For example, we used to hate and gossip, and we were jealous of others. But now, we try to speak Words of truth, praise and pray to God, and respect others. We once went to ungodly places, but now we go to church. Our homes are places to fellowship with brothers in faith.

We come to see good things and the truthful things. We don't want to hear gossip or slanderous words that are spoken out of envy, but only the Word of truth. We only want to have conversations before God in the truth.

As we change this way, our body itself becomes a beautiful house of the truth, namely the temple of God. If the truth and untruth are half and half, then in us half is controlled by the devil. It means we have built the temple 'half way'. We are building the temple of God in us to the extent that we struggle against and cast away sins to the point of shedding blood and clothe ourselves with the truth.

When we rid ourselves of all the things that are against the truth and live in the Word of God, we can be called 'spiritual men'. It means we have built the temple of God in our hearts completely. These people walk with God and communicate with Him. They are able to receive anything they ask, and they are guided in the ways of prosperity. Because they have become the holy temple of God, all tests and trials go away, and they will live with the protection of God.

The third strand of the cord concerns the church as a whole. The pastor teaches the Word of God in each church. The flock will take what they are fed and grow in spirit. Some become the pillars in the sanctuary of God, and some others play the role of the bricks, and still others act like paint, each contributing as a part of the building.

If all they do is just to attend services, then, they are like sand and the cement. Therefore, in the sight of God everyone is important because each one makes up a part of the sanctuary of God, even though they may not have any positions in the church.

Whether the positions are considered "higher" or "lower," or whether or not they have a position at all, the temple of God can be built only when each one does his/her part. Those who are like supporting pillars have to fulfill their duty as the pillars of the building since the structure would collapse without pillars.

In addition to the pillars, there are bricks and cement, and the painting of the walls. All are important. If the paint is stripped off just a little bit, it looks ugly. The temple of God can be built wonderfully when each one plays his/her part properly. These are the three-strands of the cord in the verse.

Verse 10 says, "According to the grace of God which was given to me, like a wise master builder I laid a foundation."

Here, the foundation refers to Jesus Christ. To be spiritually wise, a person receives wisdom from God, not from this world or through any education.

What is this God-given wisdom? It is to rejoice always, pray without ceasing, and give thanks in all circumstances. It is also the wisdom and will of God to live in the Word of God, cast away all forms of evil, and become sanctified.

Like a wise master builder, we have to build on our foundations with the Word of truth of Jesus Christ. Namely, we have to keep the Word of God to become a man of spirit.

To build a building we need the construction tools and equipment and building materials like cement, bricks, and wood. But, what do we need to build the temple of God?

We must have our 'selves.' That is, we must have our hearts, our minds, and our souls. Then, we have to fill each of them with the Word of truth. Also, we can build our temple only when the Holy Spirit does His job acting as the equipment needed for building.

What are the materials needed to build our temple? When we sing praises, we are filled with faith, grace, and love for God. Through prayers, we can receive the help of the Holy Spirit to overcome the world and cast away what is against the truth. Keeping the Word of God, praising God, and prayers become the materials to build the temple of God.

Then verse 10 continues, "and another is building on it. But each man must be careful how he builds on it."

Suppose the pastor of the church, like the wise master builder Paul, is teaching the Word of God on the foundation of Jesus Christ. His co-pastors and workers will also become wise in leading the flock to the truth. This way, they will have a temple, a sanctuary of God in the sense of the three-strand cord.

But now let's consider another situation. Suppose the pastor teaches well with the Word of God, but other workers in the church use their own thoughts when feeding the flock. Then it is like building a house on sand. Even though the foundation is very strong, if we build the first floor with sand and add a second floor on top of it, it will collapse.

The person who is building on the foundation is also important. Therefore, the workers in the church as well as the pastor have to receive the Word properly and build the house, or it will be only like a house built on sand.

We must not build the temple, the sanctuary of God, with human thoughts. We have to clearly hear the voice of the Holy Spirit to be able to build the complete temple.

For no man can lay a foundation other than the one which is laid, which is Jesus Christ. (3:11)

After laying the foundation on Jesus Christ who is the rock, we must not add any other foundation to it. That is why verse 10 tells us to be careful. Namely, we must not add any human knowledge or any other contents that are based on men's theory. We can build the complete temple of God only when we build upon Jesus Christ, the Rock of the Truth.

Each One's Work

**Now if any man builds on the foundation with gold,
silver, precious stones, wood, hay, straw, (3:12)**

The foundation, as previously explained, refers to the Lord.
Men build the house on the foundation of Jesus Christ. Some
build up with gold, some others with silver, and still others will
build with precious stones, wood, hay, or straw.

Gold does not react chemically with any other substances.
So, it keeps its glitter and as an element it does not change.
It can be used for various purposes, for it can be molded into
various shapes.

Of course some may think that jewels are more precious
than gold. But jewels cannot be used for multiple purposes
like gold. Diamond, sapphire, emerald, and other gemstones
may have beautiful color and glitter, but they are worthless
once they are broken. Silver is much weaker in value and less

beautiful than gold. God considers gold most valuable, next silver, and precious stones, according to their usages.

Revelation 4:2-3 says, *"Immediately I was in the Spirit; and behold, a throne was standing in heaven, and One sitting on the throne. And He who was sitting was like a jasper stone and a sardius in appearance."* It compares the image of God with a jasper and a sardius. This is just a comparison to express the beauty of God. But in the passage above the most valuable is gold, then silver, and then precious stones.

Following the metals and gemstones appear wood, hay, and lastly straw. Paul likened our faith to gold, silver, precious stones, and wood, hay, and lastly straw.

> **...each man's work will become evident; for the day will show it because it is to be revealed with fire, and the fire itself will test the quality of each man's work. (3:13)**

What is meant by the expression 'each man's work'?

Here, 'each man's work' is what each of us does with all our heart, mind, and strength to give to God. Our faith can be categorized into six different classifications according to what kind of heart, mind, and soul we have given to God and how much we live in the Word of God. Some have the faith of gold. Others have the faith of silver, which is a little less than the faith of gold. Still others have faith of precious stones, wood, hay, or straw.

The depth and magnitude of faith are different from the faith of gold to the faith of straw. Through the class of faith that is like the faith of hay, we have the faith to receive salvation. But if we have the faith of straw, we cannot receive salvation.

What Is Meant by 'the Day'?

Our work will become evident on 'the day' according to what we have done. Then, to which day is it that 'the day' referring?

First, it is the day of the evaluation of how well we have fulfilled our duties.

It is the end of each year. When we have a duty to serve in the church, some bear a lot of fruit at the end of the year while some others do not produce much.

At the end of the year, we can clearly see how much each one fasted and prayed, offered their time and financial support, and gave love to others for the kingdom and righteousness of God. As our work becomes evident, we will receive the rewards in the kingdom of Heaven.

Suppose a pastor has prayed hard and provided the church members with spiritual care. But at the end of the year, there aren't really any works being evidenced. He tried hard, but in fact, he remained as he was a year ago. Consequently, he doesn't gain any commendation or any rewards from God.

A layman member may think, "Since pastors do the work of the Lord all day, they store up their rewards, but we laymen members will probably have only a few rewards in Heaven." But this is not right. When pastors do not show any work that can be acknowledged by God, they will receive no reward. It is their duty to save the souls and take care of them, and therefore, they have to show a very clear evidence of their work.

However, whether they are students in their studies or businessmen in their businesses, laymen members who have faith can do whatever they do for the glory of God. Even when they expand their knowledge or work to gain wealth and fame, they do it all for the glory of God. They work hard for their businesses and in their workplaces, and then they use their income to do and support missionary works and charitable works for the kingdom of God.

Therefore, God also evaluates the works of the laymen members who have secular jobs in the world. If they fulfill their duties faithfully as laymen members and give honor to God in their lives, it means their works are revealed clearly in the sight of God, and thus they can receive reward. God searches everybody and measures precisely in His justice. He appraises the works of those who show the work of gold, of silver, or of wood.

Secondly, 'the day' refers to the time of fiery trials.

When we face tests and trials, we show our faith before

God. Some show the faith of gold, some others faith of silver, and still others faith of precious stones or even wood, hay, or straw.

What if a person who has the faith of gold faces a great trial? He will never be shaken or fall even facing great problems. Even if gold is broken into pieces, we can mold it to the original shape again. Those who have such faith will stand up again in difficulties, even though they may seem to be falling for a moment. They do not complain against God in any situation but rather rejoice and give thanks to Him.

Who were some of the people in the Bible who had the faith of gold?

Peter, the disciple of Jesus, kept his righteousness in God. Even as he was being crucified upside down, he was preaching the gospel of Jesus Christ. Of course, at one time he had denied the Lord three times, but it was before he had received the Holy Spirit. But from the time he received the Holy Spirit, he was faithful to the point of death.

Let us also consider the Virgin Mary who bore Jesus by the Holy Spirit. Luke 1:31-33 says, *"And behold, you will conceive in your womb and bear a son, and you shall name Him Jesus. He will be great and will be called the Son of the Most High; and the Lord God will give Him the throne of His father David; and He will reign over the house of Jacob forever, and His kingdom will have no end."*

This is what the archangel Gabriel told the Virgin Mary

about the birth of Jesus. To this, she answered, *"Behold, the bondslave of the Lord; may it be done to me according to your word"* (v. 38).

According to the Law, a person would be stoned if he or she was found to have committed adultery. If Mary became pregnant, people would have judged her to have committed adultery. But Mary was not afraid and just obeyed. She had the faith of gold.

The apostle Paul also had an unchanging heart. From the time when he too met the Lord, he preached the gospel to the Gentiles until his death.

Acts 16:25 says, *"But about midnight Paul and Silas were praying and singing hymns of praise to God, and the prisoners were listening to them."* He was imprisoned because of preaching the gospel, but he didn't complain against God. He just praised and prayed to Him.

He rejoiced and gave thanks even in harsh sufferings. Because he had the faith of gold, he was able to serve the Lord without sparing even his life.

Those who have the faith of silver have faith that is just a little less than those who have the faith of gold, but they also have great faith.

Then, what about those who have the faith of precious gemstones? When people are filled with God's grace or when they are healed of a disease by God's power, they may make up their minds and profess that they will dedicate themselves to God and diligently preach the gospel. People may also say that they want to live for God alone when their prayers are answered.

When these people with faith like gemstones do as they profess, they appear to have faith of gold. But they don't really have it. When faced with trials their hearts and their minds will change. They seem to have faith when they are full of the Holy Spirit, but when that fullness is gone, their faith breaks down and their hearts change. This is the faith like precious gemstones that may look beautiful for a time, but can be broken. Then, what about the faith of wood, hay, or straw? Such faith is worthless because all three will be consumed by fiery tests of refinement.

Thirdly, at the Lord's Second Coming the believers will be caught up in the air and after that there is a final judgment day in which all believers receive their just rewards from God. It is in this final day of God's judgment that we have the third meaning of 'the day.'

On this Day of Judgment, God will accurately measure how faithful and sanctified we have been while living on this earth, and give us the rewards according to the result of the judgment.

If any man's work which he has built on it remains, he will receive a reward. (3:14)

The faith of gold, silver, and precious gemstones will have

something that remains after the test of the refining fire. Their usages and hardness are different, but gold, silver, and precious stones are not burned by fire. The most unchanging and enduring among the three is gold, and next is silver, and next is the precious gemstones.

But unlike gold, silver, and precious stones, wood, hay, and straw will be burned by the fire in the fiery tests. Those who have the remains of their works like gold, silver, and precious gemstones will receive their reward. Faith that is anything less will not have any reward to receive.

If they fulfill their duties on this earth, they will receive the reward of acknowledgment for their work. Even if they don't receive anything on earth, they are recognized by God and brothers in faith. Also, they will have the rewards stored in Heaven.

If we show the faith of gold, silver, or precious stones in tests and trials, it means we have passed the test, and God will not only bless us but also give us rewards at the Final Judgment. We will receive the rewards according to what remains from our work after trials.

If any man's work is burned up, he will suffer loss; but he himself will be saved, yet so as through fire. (3:15)

Faith like wood, hay, or straw may have nothing left after being refined in fire. For example, you may have worked hard as a cell leader, but you had no fruit and did not have any revival of the group. It infers that the character of your faith was not hot enough; that is, it was lukewarm.

In Revelation 3:15-16 the Lord rebuked the church of Laodicea for having lukewarm faith. Our Lord wants our faith to grow hotter day after day to bear much fruit.

What does the Bible tell us about those who are lukewarm and do not fulfill their duties? From Matthew 25:15-30 the parable of the talents is recorded. When the one who received five talents produced five talents more, the Lord commended him saying, *"Well done, good and faithful slave. You were faithful with a few things, I will put you in charge of many things; enter into the joy of your master"* (v. 21).

But the one who received one talent just put it away and did not do any work with it. The master said to him, "You wicked, lazy slave" and took that one talent from him and gave it to the one who had ten talents. He then drove him out. As said, "If any man's work is burned up, he will suffer loss," this person suffered the loss.

If we do not make a concerted effort to store up our work for God, it will be a loss for the kingdom of God. If a cell leader does not fulfill her duties, the cell members will suffer a loss; their souls won't prosper; and they won't be able to avoid trials.

Likewise, if the pastor does not do his duty, then, the whole congregation will suffer the loss; their faith will be weakened; and some of them will stumble in faith or face many tests and trials.

If this happens, God has little choice but to rebuke them. They may yet be saved but it will be as through the refining fire. It means they can still be saved because they did not lose their faith and they worked for God, but just barely. They can receive only shameful salvation without receiving any rewards.

Destroying the Temple of God

Do you not know that you are a temple of God and
***that* the Spirit of God dwells in you? (3:16)**

'You' here does not only refer to the believers in the church of Corinth but also all children of God. Are you a temple of God? Have you received the Holy Spirit?

God's temple is the body of the Lord. The Holy Spirit dwells in the hearts of those who have accepted Jesus Christ as their Savior. The Holy Spirit moves our hearts to live in the truth and He guides us to the kingdom of Heaven. We are called the temple of God because the Holy Spirit is dwelling in us.

Then, why did Paul reprimand them saying, "Do you not know that you are a temple of God and that the Spirit of God dwells in you?"

The apostle Paul taught the members of the church in Corinth not to become fleshly men but become spiritual men.

Spiritual men are those who realize the Word of truth, keep it in mind, and practice it. They are the ones who pray, worship, and practice the truth according to the Word of God.

We can have faith like gold if we cast off all forms of evil and do good, not telling lies in following the Word. We have to have faith like at least that of silver or precious stones. But the members in the church of Corinth did not have such faith, and that is why Paul reprimanded them.

> **If any man destroys the temple of God, God will destroy him, for the temple of God is holy, and that is what you are. (3:17)**

Paul says, "If anyone destroys the temple of God, God will destroy him." This verse applies to all believers. Unbelievers have nothing to do with God anyway for they are children of the devil. We don't have to talk about them for they have nothing to do with salvation.

Today, many people do not correctly teach this clearly stated Word of God. Some say, "We will receive salvation once we receive the Holy Spirit. Once we are saved we are always saved. So, even though we commit sins, we will receive salvation anyway. It is because God will guide us in some way, even by punishing us, so we will receive salvation." But this is wrong. Even though we have received the Holy Spirit, if we willfully commit sins, the Holy Spirit will be extinguished, in which case the soul cannot be saved (Hebrews 10:26; 1 Thessalonians

5:19).

What does it mean by destroying the temple of God? The temple is where God is enthroned, and so, it refers to defiling our heart where the Holy Spirit is dwelling.

Then, where is our heart? We have a spiritual body inside us that looks just like us, and our "heart" is all of this spiritual body. In the heart we have conscience. The conscience is the standard of judgment that one forms for a period of time. It is the basis on which we determine right and wrong.

A newborn baby does not have a conscience. Who would say to a baby who has been crying all night long, "What is the matter with you, don't you even have conscience"? Children plant what they see, hear, learn, and realize into their hearts as they grow. Such things add up to become their conscience and their standard of judgment.

If they learn that it's manlier to hit back when they have been struck by somebody, then, it will become their standard in judging the value of recourse in such a situation. But many parts of this conscience are not correct according to the Word of God.

Therefore, everything that we have put in our heart that is against the truth must be cast off. We must then plant the Word of God in us instead of the untruth. We have to get rid of the untruths like falsehood, hatred, judging and condemnation and then follow the truth.

When we cast off the untruth and follow the truth, our

heart that is the temple of God, will be clean. If not, then the evil remains in us, and God says that we will perish since we are unclean.

But we shouldn't think that we will perish just because we still have sins that we haven't been able to cast away yet. We may have some sins left in our hearts, but if we are continuously trying to cast them away, God is pleased with such acts.

For example, suppose there is a very hot-tempered person. But he listens to the Word of truth, realizes that he is a sinner, and reduces through prayers the number of times he gets angry. God will not say he is a sinner. God believes that this person will keep on changing and someday become a person who never gets angry.

But if somebody does not try to cast off the hot-temper knowing that it is sin, God will turn His back on such a person. This proves that he has no faith. If one truly believes, he will definitely struggle against sins to cast them away.

It's the same with hatred, envy, jealousy, strife, and judging. As we discover the things that are not right before God and try to get rid of them through fervent prayers, our heart, which is the temple of the Holy Spirit, will become holy and we will shine with the truth.

Worldly Wisdom is Foolish

Let no man deceive himself. If any man among you thinks that he is wise in this age, he must become foolish, so that he may become wise. (3:18)

God advises us not to deceive ourselves. To deceive ourselves is to deceive our hearts, and this is trying to deceive the Holy Spirit in us, which is the same as trying to deceive God.

What does it mean "to deceive ourselves"? Deceiving ourselves is to know the Word of God, but not practicing it. People who deceive themselves are actually trying to deceive God. They find no joy in trying to lead their lives in faith. They are unable to sense that the Word of God is sweet as honey. They just attend church with a vague hope that they will someday live in the truth.

But the Bible tells us that the Lord is coming back soon, and we don't know when God will take our spirits. We should not just hope that we will change someday. We have to make up our mind to practice the Word from the moment we hear it.

The verse continues to say, "If any man among you thinks that he is wise in this age, he must become foolish, so that he may become wise."

Anyone who thinks that he is wise according to the wisdom of the world is arrogant before God. Such people will not receive the Word of God because of their arrogance, and this will lead them to destruction. They cannot believe the Word of God because they put their wisdom first before the wisdom of God. They try to discern the Word of God within their thoughts and by their wisdom. Thus, we have to set aside and even destroy this kind of wisdom of the world if it conflicts with the wisdom of God.

As explained earlier, this does not mean we have to forget the knowledge that we gained in this world. It means that worldly wisdom and knowledge cannot lead us to the way of life. Only the Lord is the way, truth, and life. The knowledge of this world is merely information that we need to continue our lives on earth. It can never guide us to the way of eternal life.

The verse also tells us to "become foolish." It means we have to open our hearts, become like children, and practice the Word when we receive it. We have to have the humble, simple, and pure hearts of children. When we become spiritual children this way, we will forsake our own wisdom, receive the wisdom from above, and go the way of eternal life.

Things on earth will perish and the wisdom of the world cannot lead us to eternal life. That is why the verse says it is wise to cast off the wisdom of the world that is not in accordance with the Word of God, to become "foolish," and to live by the Word of God.

> **For the wisdom of this world is foolishness before God. For it is written, '*He is* the one who catches the wise in their craftiness'; and again, 'The Lord knows the reasonings of the wise, that they are useless.' (3:19-20)**

In Luke 16, we see a rich man who enjoyed himself everyday partying in colorful clothes, but went down to the Lower Grave(Hades) after his death, suffering from the flames, being unable to get even a drop of water. He might have seemed to be wise while he was alive, but when he went down to the Lower Grave, he couldn't even get a drop of water. How painful it is! And he has to continue such a life forever, and how foolish this is!

Those who think they have wisdom will fall in their craftiness. Craftiness means 'To be adept in the use of subtlety and cunning.' As they are caught by their own craftiness, they say such foolish things as, "Where is God?" They don't even seek God believing in their own wisdom, and finally they go the way of destruction.

Next, it says, "The Lord knows the reasonings of the wise, that they are useless." Even though we may learn many things to become a scientist or a medical doctor, invent many things, or earn great fortunes, it is nothing in the sight of God.

Ecclesiastes 1:2-3 says, *"'Vanity of vanities,' says the Preacher, 'Vanity of vanities! All is vanity.' What advantage does man have in all his work which he does under the sun?"* And Verse 14 says, *"I have seen all the works which have been done under the sun, and behold, all is vanity and striving after wind."*

Even though we have gained many things with our effort and toil, it is useless because only Hell awaits us if we do not know God. But if we have life in us, we will give glory to God in all things. It is not useless but worthy for our way is headed for the eternal kingdom of Heaven.

So then let no one boast in men. For all things belong to you, (3:21)

God says, "let no one boast in men." Believers have nothing to boast but Christ. One might have great wisdom and he may be very famous, but all these things are also useless if he has no life in him. That is why Jesus loved tax collectors and prostitutes rather than high priests or elders who had wisdom.

In Matthew 21:31 Jesus talked with high priests and some others. It says, *"Truly I say to you that the tax collectors and prostitutes will get into the kingdom of God before you."*

The priests and elders could not receive the Word because

they were arrogant and had pride in themselves thinking that they possessed wisdom. They were not even able to recognize the Savior who was standing in front of them. But the tax collectors and prostitutes realized their sins, repented, and received salvation. Therefore, boasting is useless, and we have to boast only in the Lord.

The verse also says, "for all things belong to you." All things belong to God, and they also belong to us for He is our Father. God will give them to us when all things are recovered.

If the truth dwells in a person and his soul is prosperous, all things belong to him in this world, too. It's because all things will be done as he desires in heart as said in Psalm 37:4, *"Delight yourself in the LORD; and He will give you the desires of your heart."* God considers us as His temple. So, if we resemble Him by having a holy and clean temple in us, then, all things belong to us.

whether Paul or Apollos or Cephas or the world or life or death or things present or things to come; all things belong to you, and you belong to Christ; and Christ belongs to God. (3:22-23)

Paul, Apollos, and Cephas, who is more commonly called Peter, were all servants of God. Since all were servants, it was not necessary for there to be any divisions among the believers. Also, the world belongs to us for it belongs to God the Father. Also, death is in us because all bodies die once.

Spiritually, too, we go the way of life by believing in Jesus Christ. If we leave God, death will come to us again. So, life or death all depend on us and belong to us. Things present or things to come also belong to us.

The verse also says that we belong to Christ, and Christ belongs to God. Everything is created by Jesus Christ (Colossians 1:16). When we belong to Jesus Christ, and Jesus Christ belongs to God, then all believers belong to God. Because all things belong to God, they also belong to us!

Requirements of Servants Who Are Stewards

Let a man regard us in this manner, as servants of Christ and stewards of the mysteries of God. In this case, moreover, it is required of stewards that one be found trustworthy (4:1-2).

Here the term 'a man' refers to both believers and unbelievers. Then, who are the servants of Christ? First, they are those who give out the fragrance of Christ as the servants of Christ and stewards of the mysteries of God.

Also, whoever has a duty or title in the church is a servant of Christ. But even those who do not have a title or a position in the church have a duty as children of God and they also have to give out the fragrance of Christ.

Who are the stewards of the mysteries of God? 'Mystery' here refers to the way of the cross. 1 Corinthians 2:7 says, *"but we speak God's wisdom in a mystery, the hidden wisdom which*

God predestined before the ages to our glory." It is a mystery because it was hidden before the ages.

Adam was created as a living spirit, but his spirit died due to his disobedience. Since then, all mankind was destined to death, which is the wage of sin. But the God of love prepared Jesus Christ before the ages to open the way of salvation.

This mystery was revealed on the cross through Jesus Christ about 2,000 years ago. The Bible has many secrets that lead us to the way of life. Those who realize these secrets are referred to as 'stewards of the mysteries of God.'

In verse 2, the 'stewards' are the stewards of the mysteries of God. As they learn the Word of God, they realize and understand the command of the Lord telling us to preach the gospel to all nations and all peoples. They also take part and contribute as the Sunday school teachers, choir members, deacons, senior deaconesses, and elders.

Thus, we should not only fulfill the duty of preaching but also the duties in the church. God promised that He would give the crown of life to those who are faithful until death (Revelation 2:10).

To be faithful is to give all our hearts, minds, souls, and even our lives to fulfill our duties. When a paid worker just does his job, we cannot say he is faithful. We can say he is faithful only when he does more than what he is supposed to do not sparing his money and time.

How Is a Man Justified?

**But to me it is a very small thing that I may be
examined by you, or by *any* human court; in fact, I
do not even examine myself. For I am conscious of
nothing against myself, yet I am not by this acquitted;
but the one who examines me is the Lord. (4:3-4)**

If somebody examines and judges you, is it something big or
small? If somebody is judging you, it means he is violating the
Word of God, and he is evil. A man of truth will obey the Word
of God and not pass judgment and condemnation nor criticize
others.

An evil person may judge you though you are living in the
Word of God, but this is a small thing for you. God doesn't say
you are a sinner for you did not violate the truth. Satan cannot
accuse you either. You don't have anything to repent.

But then, why did the apostle Paul say it was a 'small thing' and not say that it was 'nothing'?

Luke 6:27-28 says, *"But I say to you who hear, love your enemies, do good to those who hate you, bless those who curse you, pray for those who mistreat you."*

It is a 'small thing' for you because there is no accusation that can be brought against you, but the accuser who judged you acted with his evil. But you still need to pray for him with love so he won't go the way of destruction. Paul said that it was 'small thing', not 'nothing' because he also had to pray for such people.

Verse 4 says, "For I am conscious of nothing against myself, yet I am not by this acquitted; but the one who examines me is the Lord." If we live by the Word of God, then we won't have anything that would bring accusation against us. It means our lives pass the evaluation of the seven Spirits.

These 'seven Spirits' represent the heart of God that searches the seven aspects of people's lives. These aspects are faith, joy, prayer, thanks, keeping the commandments, faithfulness, and love. The seven Spirits examine whether we live by the Word, and to receive the answer to our prayers, we have to pass the evaluation (Revelation 5:6).

If we are living in the Word of God when measured by the seven Spirits, then we won't be conscious of anything against ourselves.

But why did Paul say, "yet I am not by this acquitted"? Men can be justified only through faith in Jesus Christ. This is done only by the grace of God (Galatians 2:16; Romans 10:10). Romans 3:23-24 says, *"For all have sinned and fall short of the glory of God, being justified as a gift by His grace through the redemption which is in Christ Jesus."*

We cannot be justified without faith. We cannot be joy to God either. Even though we help others and we are sincere in our service, we cannot receive any rewards without faith.

Only God can measure our faith. Men judge with the outward deeds and they cannot judge correctly. For example, they may just think somebody has great faith because he works diligently in the church.

But if he's not able to overcome a test or trial and returns to the way of the world, what he did was not done by faith. If he really had faith, he couldn't leave God but bear fruit according to that faith. Men likewise judge by only things that can be seen and cannot make proper judgment. Only God can make precise judgment of the heart.

Also, men make wrong judgments because they judge with wisdom and the value of the world that is against the truth. This is the same as measuring something with a broken measure or inaccurate scale. Only God measures most precisely for He searches the heart with the standard of the truth. As said, "...but the one who examines me is the Lord," only the Lord, and God can examine justly and correctly.

Therefore do not go on passing judgment before the time, but wait until the Lord comes who will both bring to light the things hidden in the darkness and disclose the motives of men's hearts; and then each man's praise will come to him from God (4:5).

"Before the time, until the Lord comes" refers to the time of the Lord's Second Coming in the air. "Things hidden in the darkness" are sins and things against the truth. All these things will be revealed when the Lord comes in the air. Those who are in the darkness will not be caught up to the air. Also, among those who are caught up in the air, the holiness and blamelessness of each one's heart will be revealed clearly before the Lord.

What are the 'motives of men's hearts'? This is the motive of the Lord's heart, which is the truth. When the Lord comes back in the air, each one will receive his praise according to his deeds. He will be praised according to how much he has loved God, how faithful he been, and how much he preached the gospel and prayed.

It says, "Do not go on passing judgment until the Lord comes." The churches face tests because the members pass judgment on each other and become jealous. The Bible many times tells us it is not right to pass judgment on our brothers.

Do Not Exceed the Word

Now these things, brethren, I have figuratively applied to myself and Apollos for your sakes, so that in us you may learn not to exceed what is written, so that no one of you will become arrogant in behalf of one against the other (4:6).

The apostle Paul and Apollos taught the Word of God and set the good example themselves. Only the Word of God is the true will of God, and they didn't want anybody to be deceived by any other books or teachings that had falsehood.

What specifically did Paul and Apollos teach the believers? They taught that Jesus came to solve the problem of our sins and lead us in the way of eternal life and salvation. They emphasized that those children of God who believed this fact had to live a godly life according to the Word to receive salvation.

But some people opposed this teaching. To oppose God is

not living in the truth and following personal ideas without regard for the Word of God.

We have to keep the Sabbath holy, but they think they can just do what they want on Sundays after attending morning service only. The Bible tells us to cry out in prayer, but they think praying in silence is better and do not cry out.

When David violated the Word of God, the prophet rebuked him saying he despised the Word of the LORD God. If we do what we want according to our will, it is opposing God's will.

One who opposes God is naturally arrogant. He thinks his knowledge and ideas are correct, and he opposes the Word of God. He has become the judge in the place of God, and how arrogant it is! Proverbs 16:18 says, *"Pride goes before destruction, and a haughty spirit before stumbling."*

For who regards you as superior? What do you have that you did not receive? And if you did receive it, why do you boast as if you had not received it? You are already filled, you have already become rich, you have become kings without us; and indeed, *I* wish that you had become kings so that we also might reign with you (4:7-8).

Paul asks the believers in the Corinthian church as to who it was that divided them to be of Apollos, Paul, Cephas, or Christ, and who set one member of the church to be higher or lower than any other. Here, 'dividing' is done in arrogance. Strife and division are the works of Satan.

Then, what did God divide? He divided sins and righteousness, death and eternal life, and the darkness and the light. God divided the truth and untruth. God did not divide the members into factions of one group following one person and others following another nor did He set any individual higher than anybody else.

In essence, Paul said to the members of the Corinthian church who did not follow his teachings, "I taught to you the truth, and what is it that you did not receive? I taught you by showing you an example. But, you act like you did not receive the truth."

Also, he said, "And if you did receive it, why do you boast as if you had not received it?" Here Paul is saying that the members of the Corinthian church were not living in righteousness and acting just like the worldly people. He was saying that they were receiving works of Satan. Regarding their boasting he asked how there could be boasting among them of worldly things when God's children must boast only in the Lord, not of worldly things.

If we try to live in the truth then we should hunger and thirst for righteousness. Consider how thirsty we can become when we sweat profusely on a hot summer day. There are soldiers who would drink from any pond on the ground when they become so thirsty after hard training sessions. They don't care even if it's not clean, because it's just unbearable to hold their thirst.

Furthermore, if we are thirsty and hungry for truth we have to become humble and serve others. But the believers in the church of Corinth loved the world more than learning the truth. They were arrogant and boasting of the knowledge, wealth, and wisdom of the world that they had gained.

So, verse 8 says, "You are already filled, you have already become rich, you have become kings without us." How arrogant were these Corinthians who thought that they had become like kings! They were not hungry and thirsty for righteousness with poor hearts but instead they were filled and rich. Their actions were contrary to the truth.

There is an order in the church established by God. But, the Corinthian church members acted like they were kings. That is why Paul is rebuking them and saying they act like they did not receive any truth. If we don't have the deeds following after hearing the Word, then we have dead faith.

So, when will we reign like kings?

Revelation 20:6 says, *"Blessed and holy is the one who has a part in the first resurrection; over these the second death has no power, but they will be priests of God and of Christ and will reign with Him for a thousand years."*

Those who have accepted Jesus Christ as their Savior will be caught up in the air at the Second Coming of the Lord. They will have the Wedding Banquet in the air for 7 years. Then, when this is over, they will come down to this earth in the Millennium Kingdom to reign with the Lord.

Paul, thinking of this, said, "...and indeed, I wish that you had become kings so that we also might reign with you." He is advising the believers of Corinth that they must not act like kings in order for them to be saved and reign like kings in the Millennium Kingdom.

The apostle Paul was a person who lived in the truth knowing the true will of God and who clearly realized the way of salvation and eternal life. Therefore, Paul was the one who had to act like a king leading the believers to live in the truth. But the members of Corinthian church were arrogant and they were reigning like kings saying "this is only just," and "that is only right."

Then, they would have nothing to do with the apostle Paul, and that is why Paul is telling them they wouldn't be able to reign like kings in the Millennium Kingdom if they kept on acting like that.

Paul is saying that what he is teaching is the truth, and only when they received it and practiced it, would they be caught up in the air and reign in the Millennium Kingdom.

For, I think, God has exhibited us apostles last of all, as men condemned to death; because we have become a spectacle to the world, both to angels and to men (4:9).

There are two kinds of thoughts. One is the spiritual thought and the other is fleshly thought. When the truth in a man's heart is utilized and made as thought, it is spiritual thought. Those who live in the Word of God, namely who are spiritual men will continually have spiritual thoughts by receiving the inspiration of the Holy Spirit in their hearts. On the other hand, those who are not in the truth will first utilize the untruth in their heart through the thought coming from Satan. This is fleshly thought.

Paul said, "I think" and here, it is not human thought but spiritual thought. It's not his personal opinion but the inspiration of the Holy Spirit. Here, his 'thinking' was the truth.

An apostle is a servant of God who is fulfilling the will of God. The Bible also teaches us the way of a true servant. 1 Kings 19:21 says, *"So [Elisha] returned from following [Elijah], and took the pair of oxen and sacrificed them and boiled their flesh with the implements of the oxen, and gave it to the people and they ate. Then he arose and followed Elijah and ministered to him."*

How was it with the disciples of Jesus? Matthew 4:18-22 tells us that when Jesus called John and James as His disciples they left their boat, the net, and even their father and followed Jesus. In Galatians 1:16, Paul says that he did not 'consult with flesh and blood' when Jesus called him as His apostle.

Likewise, a true servant of God has to completely obey the

Word. He has to obey God completely and act in His will to become a holy and sanctified man of spirit. Then, he will receive power from God.

Also, even though you are not pastors or ministers, if anybody just follows the will of God completely, God will recognize you as spiritual apostles. Such persons will manifest the powerful works of God. Two examples are Philip and Stephen.

Paul continues to say, "God has exhibited us apostles last of all, as men condemned to death; because we have become a spectacle to the world, both to angels and to men."

Today, when a convict is executed, a little bit of goodness is shown to him by giving him clothes and cigarettes and asking him what his last wish is. But at the time of early churches, they maltreated and even tortured convicts who were sentenced to death. People did not treat them humanely.

They made them the prey of hungry lions, despised them, spat on them, and stoned them. The apostles were beheaded or crucified. Others were tied to decaying corpses until they also died while smelling the foul odor. The pain and sorrow must have been great.

The apostles knew about their ends. They knew they were going to die a wretched death after testifying to the resurrection of Jesus Christ. That is why Paul said, "God has exhibited us apostles last of all, as men condemned to death; because we have become a spectacle to the world, both to angels and to men."

Who controls this world? It is God. He controls it through His angels. So, not only God but angels knew when the apostle Paul and other disciples would be killed while they were receiving mockery and malice.

People would make fun of the apostles saying, "You were showing signs and wonders, and why can't you save yourself from this misery?" Paul also became a spectacle of the people when he died.

Then, what did Paul, Peter, and other apostles feel before their death?

They knew how they were going to die. Peter knew he was going to be crucified upside down. Paul knew he was going to be handed over to the Gentiles if he went up to Jerusalem. But he just took that way without fear because he knew it was the will of God (Acts 21:7-14).

God let this be recorded because the mindset of those who were going to be killed is important. What kind of feelings would they have had while doing God's work and knowing that it would bring certain death to them?

We can understand their hearts through the Bible. They gave thanks and praised God even when they were beaten. They became the prey of lions yet they rejoiced and praised God. So, what does this verse mean? In Matthew 5:11-12, the Lord says, *"Blessed are you when people insult you and persecute you, and falsely say all kinds of evil against you because of Me. Rejoice and be glad, for your reward in heaven is great; for in the same way they persecuted the prophets who were before you."*

The apostles knew this world was only momentary and meaningless. They looked up only to the rewards in Heaven. That is why they could rejoice and be glad in any situation. This is faith. How can we not rejoice when we can receive more rewards by being persecuted for the name of the Lord?

But the apostles knew when they were going to be killed, so they were nervous about time passing. It's not that they were afraid of death, but they were desperate because they wanted to save more souls within the limited time period.

That is why they fulfilled their duties with all their lives thinking that they had to show the living God to people. They had to spread the gospel and save even just one more soul.

How did Jesus act? Hebrews 12:1-2 says, *"Let us run with endurance the race that is set before us, fixing our eyes on Jesus, the author and perfecter of faith, who for the joy set before Him endured the cross, despising the shame, and has sat down at the right hand of the throne of God."*

It is such a shame that the Son of God, Jesus, was despised and mocked by His creatures and was crucified by them. How shameful it is if the master is beaten up and mocked by his own slaves?

Nevertheless, Jesus willingly took the cross for our salvation and sits on the right side of God's throne. We must also do the will of God without thinking about any shame it may bring to us.

Be Imitators of Me

We are fools for Christ's sake, but you are prudent in Christ; we are weak, but you are strong; you are distinguished, but we are without honor. (4:10)

'We' here refers to the apostle Paul, his fellow ministers Apollos, and servants of God who are acknowledged by God likewise. Furthermore, it refers to all those who have the faith to live by the will of God.

Then, why does Paul say he was a fool for Christ's sake?

It means he looked foolish in the eyes of the unbelievers or those who are supposed to be believers but did not live within the Word of God. For example, ordinary people will become angry if somebody slaps them. But those who have faith will bear with it and try to understand it even though they are innocent. It is because the Word of God tells us, when we are struck on one cheek, to turn the other cheek. Thus, we seem foolish in the eyes of the people in the world when we live within the Word of God.

Paul continues to teach the members of the Corinthian church saying, "We are fools for Christ's sake, but you are prudent in Christ."

If the members of the Corinthian church had been able to turn the left cheek when they were struck on the right by somebody, then the worldly people must have considered them foolish.

The next verse says, "we are weak, but you are strong." The apostles were weak, namely those who were living in the Word of God were weak, but those who didn't live in the truth were strong.

Paul is pointing out that, because they were not living in the truth, they thought they could do everything with their own power, but they were only making a pretense of being strong.

Let us consider the case of Jesus. In 2 Corinthians 13:4 it says, *"For indeed He was crucified because of weakness, yet He lives because of the power of God. For we also are weak in Him, yet we will live with Him because of the power of God directed toward you."*

Jesus opened the eyes of the blind, caused the lame to walk, cleansed the lepers, made the deaf hear, and even revived the dead. Moreover, He calmed down winds and waves with His Word. He was a very powerful man.

But what does it mean by, "He was crucified because of weakness"?

If Jesus had shown His power, it would have been impossible for anyone to crucify Him. On the night He was arrested, Peter cut off the ear of a servant of the high priest with his sword (Mark 14:47). But Jesus said, "Stop! No more of this." And He touched his ear and healed him. Then, Jesus reminded Peter of the fact that He could appeal to God and bring more than twelve legions of angels (Matthew 26:53).

Jesus could have driven away those people immediately if it was not God's will for Him to be arrested. Jesus had the power but He didn't use it for Himself but only to fulfill the will of God.

The Son of God Jesus is such a powerful man, but He became weak following the will of God. This was to redeem us from sins. Had He remained strong nobody would have been able to crucify Him. He became weak at God's will because we could reach salvation only if He redeemed us from our sins through His crucifixion.

Paul and other apostles also had to be weak to save the souls. Paul said, *"I was with you in weakness and in fear and in much trembling"* (1 Corinthians 2:3), and *"If I have to boast, I will boast of what pertains to my weakness"* (2 Corinthians 11:30).

Of what would you boast? Would you boast of your strength? I hope you will boast of your weakness in the Lord. If we remain strong, we will be arrogant and reveal our self-righteousness. We have to be weak in the truth to serve others humbly and consider others better than us. We have to become weak because we have to overcome evil with good.

But we have to remember one thing. Even if somebody slaps us, we should understand that person and be able to turn the other cheek. We must not allow anything that disgraces God.

In the Gospel of John 2:14-15, Jesus found people in the temple who were selling oxen, sheep and doves. There were also the money changers seated at their tables. Jesus made a scourge of cords, and drove them all out of the temple, with the sheep and the oxen; and He poured out the coins of the money changers and overturned their tables.

Jesus is meek and He is love itself, but He did not accept disgracing God by selling and buying things in the temple. Therefore, we have to understand the truth correctly and not accept anything that disgraces God or the church, which is the body of Christ.

Paul continues to say to the members of the Corinthian church, "...you are distinguished, but we are without honor." The apostles at that time were without honor indeed; they were persecuted, sometimes stoned, beaten, and despised.

Today, it's the same with faithful servants of God. If we show signs and wonders, the enemy devil will not just stay calm. He will try to hinder the works of God.

Also, some believers become jealous and disturb and cause disruption because they cannot manifest such works. God's servants or God's children may be put into very wretched situations for a variety of reasons, and it was so at the time of Paul, too.

"Are they servants of Christ?—I speak as if insane—I more so; in far more labors, in far more imprisonments, beaten times without number, often in danger of death. Five times I received from the Jews thirty-nine lashes. Three times I was beaten with rods, once I was stoned, three times I was shipwrecked, a night and a day I have spent in the deep. I have been on frequent journeys, in dangers from rivers, dangers from robbers, dangers from my countrymen, dangers from the Gentiles, dangers in the city, dangers in the wilderness, dangers on the sea, dangers among false brethren; I have been in labor and hardship, through many sleepless nights, in hunger and thirst, often without food, in cold and exposure" (2 Corinthians 11:23-27).

Usually those who are strong will beat others. But how weak and soft-witted was Paul? Because of his weakness he was beaten so many times and he received so much suffering and abuse. He was even beaten because he was without honor.

Paul was hungry, thirsty, cold, and without clothes, but he

could bear with all those things. He said that what mattered to him was only his concern for the churches.

"Apart from such external things, there is the daily pressure on me of concern for all the churches. Who is weak without my being weak? Who is led into sin without my intense concern? If I have to boast, I will boast of what pertains to my weakness" (2 Corinthians 11:28-30).

Paul boasted of his weakness. We should also boast of weakness, not strength.

To this present hour we are both hungry and thirsty, and are poorly clothed, and are roughly treated, and are homeless; and we toil, working with our own hands; when we are reviled, we bless; when we are persecuted, we endure; when we are slandered, we try to conciliate; we have become as the scum of the world, the dregs of all things, *even* until now (4:11-13).

"Being hungry and thirsty" here has a spiritual meaning. It is not about physical hunger and thirst. They were not hungry or thirsty because God failed to provide for them.

For example, there are some believers who are hungry and thirsty even though they are materially wealthy. These believers do not spend for themselves but try their best to give to God and for His kingdom, for missionary works, and church construction and so on.

Paul was preaching while working at a job. At that time the gospel was not spread at all, and he had to establish churches in a time when people were put to death for just believing in Jesus Christ. Because he had to spread the gospel in places where they didn't know Jesus Christ at all, nobody welcomed him.

That is why the apostle Paul spread the gospel making a living at the same time. But when he was reviled, he blessed, and when he was persecuted, he endured.

To be reviled is to be subject to verbal abuse. The Bible tells us to rejoice and be glad when we are persecuted for the Lord (Matthew 5:11-12).

Matthew 5:44 says, *"But I say to you, love your enemies and pray for those who persecute you."* Thus we have to love our enemies and pray for those who persecute us.

Verse 13 says, "...when we are slandered, we try to conciliate." This means when others slander us, we should guide them in understanding with good words. We should not malign and insult them, but love them, bless them, and help them understand.

Then, we will have peace, avoiding any work of Satan. Also, we will be at peace, so we can rejoice and give thanks. We should not become offended or become discouraged by anybody.

When apostles acted this way, they became as the scum of the world, the dregs of all things. What does this mean?

People raise pet dogs or pet birds with much care feeding them. Those who like plants or flowers catch the worms, water them and fertilize the soil, and pull out the weeds. They love these plants because they bring a little bit of joy and peace to the minds of the people.

But apostles were reviled, persecuted, cursed, and beaten rather than receiving love. They were treated like the scum and dregs of the world. Even animals or plants were loved and cared for by people, but the apostles were treated like rubbish.

They should have been loved more for they resolved many difficult problems of the people. They preached the Word and healed their sicknesses. But instead of being appreciated, they were beaten and condemned as heretics. They had to be constantly on the move to escape persecution. That is why Paul said they were like scum and dregs of the world.

I do not write these things to shame you, but to admonish you as my beloved children. For if you were to have countless tutors in Christ, yet *you would* not *have* many fathers, for in Christ Jesus I became your father through the gospel (4:14-15).

The apostle Paul now explains the reason why he writes this letter. It was not to shame the believers in the Corinthian church but to admonish them like his beloved children as a spiritual father.

Verse 15 says, "For if you were to have countless tutors in Christ, yet *you would* not *have* many fathers, for in Christ Jesus I became your father through the gospel."

A 'father' will feed his children, become their guardian, and educate them until they grow up. He will provide his children with the necessities of life. Since they are not a 'father', teachers are only responsible for teaching.

In the same way, today there are many teachers in the church, but not many fathers. Namely, there are many pastors who teach the Word of God. However there are not many spiritual fathers who are complete men of truth who accept the responsibility for planting faith in the believers, raising them, instructing them in responsibility and leading them until they become spiritual adults.

Apostle Paul said, "I became your father through the gospel." So, does it mean Paul became the father of the believers in the Corinthian church? Yes, he did become the father of the believers in Corinth because he gave birth to them through the gospel.

A fetus is formed when semen and an ovum combine. Then, the fetus receives the nutrients from the mother to make the bones, tendons, eyes, nose, mouth, hair, and hands and feet. The mother has to take care of the child for 9 months as he matures. 'Giving birth' is not only about the actual 'delivery', but it is all these processes that are involved in raising the child.

Then, what is it to give birth through the gospel in Jesus Christ?

When we accept Jesus Christ and receive the Holy Spirit, we receive the seed of life in our heart. Just as a seed fallen in a field sprouts, blossoms with flowers, and eventually bears fruit, the seed of life fallen in our hearts begins to grow.

What kinds of processes does a believer pass through to grow up, then? Those who have just accepted the Lord and received the Holy Spirit are like new born babies. They have only a minimal measure of faith, but their faith will grow up through the Word of God. They now begin to grow up to have the faith of little children, then that of young men, and finally of fathers (1 John 2:12-14).

At first, they might not be able to understand every Word of God that they hear, but they gradually understand the Word. They take it as their spiritual bread, and change through the truth.

Before this time, their eyes saw and ears heard things of the world. Their hands did things that were not good. But now, they take delight in seeing, hearing, and doing the things that are in the truth. They try to think and plan good things and speak good words.

What can cause this kind of change to take place? They understand the Word of God preached and it changes their lives. Fleshly men become spiritual men, and this is the giving birth through the gospel that Paul spoke about.

Of course, the only father of spirit is God the Father. However we can call those who give birth to us through the gospel 'spiritual fathers.' Namely, God is our original Father, but servants of God who give birth to us through the gospel and lead us to grow up in spirit can also become our spiritual fathers. But of course the levels are different.

Therefore I exhort you, be imitators of me (4:16).

Paul said in 1 Corinthians 11:1, *"Be imitators of me, just as I also am of Christ."* There is a condition to his exhortation.

If a father can say with confidence that he has lived a successful and upright life, then how would you expect him to teach his children? He would probably teach them to take after his example.

But suppose a father didn't really live an exemplary life. He is a drunkard and a fighter. Then, he would probably have to advise his children to follow the example of somebody else who is outstanding.

The apostle Paul advised the believers in Corinth with a heart of the confident father, "Therefore I exhort you, be imitators of me." He could teach the believers in Corinth with such words because he followed after Jesus Christ.

This verse means, "Love God to the utmost degree as I love Him to the utmost degree, and be faithful until death as I have been faithful until death." How did the apostle Paul love God?

As in 2 Corinthians 11, he became foolish on account of

Christ. For Christ he became weak and without honor; he was thirsty, hungry, beaten up and without clothes, and when he was persecuted, he endured and prayed for the persecutors, and when he was reviled, he blessed them.

Paul did all these things within the truth. He could say "Be imitators of me" because he dwelt in the Word of God by loving Christ and accomplishing the characters of Jesus Christ.

Namely, if we take after Paul, it means we take after Jesus. If we take after the characters of Jesus, it means we accomplish God's characters, and furthermore participate in His divine nature (2 Peter 1:4).

This is somewhat similar to the case in which the disciples of Jesus asked Him to show God to them. Jesus replied that those who had seen Him had seen God. It's because by following only God's will Jesus resembled God. We should also be able to boldly tell others to be imitators of ourselves by loving God and living in the truth.

For this reason I have sent to you Timothy, who is my beloved and faithful child in the Lord, and he will remind you of my ways which are in Christ, just as I teach everywhere in every church (4:17).

Paul refers to Timothy as 'my beloved and faithful child in the Lord' because Paul loved Timothy very much and raised him with the Word of truth. In return, Timothy became a faithful man by following the example of the apostle Paul and living in the truth.

Paul sent Timothy in his place to Corinth to teach the believers in the church there what he had been teaching in all the churches. Here, as everywhere else and in every church, what was taught was not different, but the same. He taught the same Word of God and the same way of the cross. He testified to the resurrection of Jesus Christ and showed the evidence of the truth of the Word with his deeds.

Then, what does it mean by "Timothy will remind you of the things that Paul teaches everywhere in every church"? Timothy took after the example of Paul's deeds and taught what he had learned from Paul.

For example, the apostle Paul did not only teach that they had to pray with fasting and crying out to receive the answer from God. He practiced what he had taught. Timothy would do the same. Timothy wouldn't just teach, but demonstrated and practiced what he taught. Paul helped the poor and encouraged those who were in trials and hardships. Timothy would do the same, helping the poor and encouraging the believers in hardships.

What Timothy did was the same as what Paul did. That is why even though the apostle Paul was not with them, when they saw the actions of Timothy the believers in the church of Corinth were reminded of Paul.

Power and Ability through the Kingdom of God

> Now some have become arrogant, as though I were not coming to you. But I will come to you soon, if the Lord wills, and I shall find out, not the words of those who are arrogant but their power (4:18-19).

The apostle Paul established a church in Corinth and left on a mission trip to Asia. In the mean time, some of the believers in Corinth became arrogant. They thought Paul would never come back and they themselves came to act like kings. They did not respect those who were higher in the church order.

In fact, everyone should keep this in mind, for we have very similar cases even today. Arrogance can grow without our even being aware that it is happening. When it gets more serious, it will be revealed for others to see it, but the person himself won't be able to realize it.

Therefore, we always have to check ourselves with the Word

of God. The lower in position in the order of the church should have the respect for the higher in order. Not even the leaders should decide and do everything independently as they desire.

Verse 19 talks about the heart of Paul having a concern for the fact that the members in Corinthian church became arrogant. They were becoming obstacles for the kingdom of God, and disgracing Him. Paul wanted to visit them immediately to solve that problem, but it was not easy since he was in Ephesus.

Paul understood very well through many experiences that he couldn't do anything within his will unless the Lord allowed him. When he wanted to go to Asia to preach the gospel, the Holy Spirit stopped him. In a vision Paul had seen a Macedonian who had asked him to come to Macedonia to help them. He then changed his course and immediately headed to Europe (Acts 16:6-10).

All children of God can hear the voice of the Holy Spirit to the extent that they cast off untruths from their hearts and cultivate truth in them. Then, once we hear the voice of the Holy Spirit, we have to follow it rather than following our own thoughts.

But if we try to make the decision according to our thoughts, theories, and experiences even after hearing the voice of the Holy Spirit, then God cannot lead us to be successful. In this case, if we immediately realize that our way is not the will of God and repent and then turn away, we can avoid tests and trials for God will work for the good of everything.

But in most cases, those who do not hear or obey the voice of the Holy Spirit will keep on acting according to their own ideas and they cannot accomplish their plans completely. Even when the Holy Spirit groans in them and they feel the afflictions in their hearts, they don't take it seriously and keep on going their way. Then, they will come to face hardships.

Paul continued to say, "But I will come to you soon, if the Lord wills, and I shall find out, not the words of those who are arrogant but their power." The 'power' here is a little different from the 'power' mentioned in verse 20. Here, "I shall find out their power" means that Paul wanted to find out their deeds in truthfulness. In order for us to live by the Word of God, we have to receive the power of God that exceeds anything of our own effort.

Please think about the time when you first accepted the Lord and received God's grace. After accepting the Christ and receiving the Holy Spirit, we begin to learn the Word of God. Then, we make up our mind to live according to God's Word, but in fact we cannot just do it easily. We have the desire to follow the Word, but we don't have the strength to do it.

At this moment, we can receive grace and power from above and practice the Word of the truth one by one and step by step if we keep on praying unceasingly. But if we do not pray, we cannot receive power from above and thus cannot practice the Word, even though we have been Christians for a long time.

Thus, to lead a blessed life by keeping the Word of God, we have to pray continually. It shouldn't be the case where we pray because we are filled with the Spirit and we don't pray when we've lost the fullness of the Spirit. We should not only pray with all our hearts and without ceasing, but we must make prayer a habit.

Just as Jesus followed His habit to pray, we have to do the same to fill up the amount of our prayers. As we increase the amount of prayer, we have more spiritual communication with God. Then, our soul will be prosperous and we will receive the power to live according to the Word.

For the kingdom of God does not consist in words but in power (4:20).

The 'power' here is a little different from the power in the previous verse. The power here is a power that is at a higher level than the power in verse 19. Paul said the kingdom of God does not consist in words, but in power. Today, there is a lot of talk in many churches, but the kingdom of God is not in words but in power, and words alone are useless.

The apostles in the early churches did not have good speaking skills. Peter was originally a fisherman. He didn't have the ability to speak well and he did not have a lot of worldly knowledge, but when he received the power from above, he persuaded three thousand men to repent in one day. Paul did not have oratory skills, but he had the power of God. He laid the foundation of the world evangelization in the midst of the difficult situations in early churches.

It's the same today. God's kingdom consists of power alone. Excellent knowledge or wisdom of the world cannot save many souls. We cannot either enlarge the kingdom of God with words or wisdom of men or win the victory in the battle against the enemy devil.

We saw earlier in 1 Corinthians 2:4 that the apostle Paul said, *"My message and my preaching were not in persuasive words of wisdom, but in demonstration of the Spirit and of power."* He gained much knowledge studying under Gamaliel, but he considered it all loss and like rubbish.

Here, what is this 'power' that can plant faith in people, save the souls, and expand the kingdom of God?

First, the power is to keep and practice the Word of God in deeds and truth when we accept Jesus Christ, receive the Holy Spirit, and pray before God.

Second, it is to bear the fruit as we continue practicing the Word. We will bear the fruits of the Holy Spirit as we live by God's Word, and this cannot just be done as we desire, but only by the 'power' in faith.

When these people who bear the fruit of the Holy Spirit pray with faith to receive more power, God will give them the power and authority from above. It is the power of the Word, and the power that is followed by signs and wonders.

Even though we don't have good speech skills, we will be able to preach the Word that penetrates even to the division of spirit and soul; joints and marrow; and change the heart if we receive the power of the Word from God. We can plant faith in them and help them live in the Word of God.

In John 4:48 is recorded, *"So Jesus said to him, 'Unless you people see signs and wonders, you simply will not believe.'"*

In order to save the souls, we must have not only the power of the Word, but also manifest the signs and wonders that can plant faith in the people. People will really believe when they see the signs and wonders and the evidence that God is with them. This way, they can overcome the world and live in the Word of God.

If there are no signs and wonders, it's difficult to have true faith and live by the Word. It can only produce 'churchgoers' who are like chaff. With the development of science and technology, we are in even greater need of signs and wonders than ever before, but some people are critical about it when we say there are signs and wonders taking place.

But those who have good hearts will accept Jesus as their personal Savior when they see signs and wonders. Both at the time of Jesus and today, it is those who do not have good heart who criticize such amazing works.

In the book of Acts, we find that at the hands of the apostles many signs and wonders were taking place among the people, and the number of believers in the Lord continually increased

(Acts 5:12-14). Also, after the resurrection and ascension of Jesus Christ, the disciples went out and preached everywhere, while the Lord worked with them, and confirmed the Word by the signs that followed (Mark 16:19-20).

As above, the kingdom of God is not in words but in power. When the power is manifested, true faith is given to people, and they can stand firmly on the Word of truth and lead a life of victory.

What do you desire? Shall I come to you with a rod, or with love and a spirit of gentleness (4:21)?

Here, 'rod' refers to the punishment in reprimanding. The apostle Paul had the authority to punish some of the believers in the Corinthian church, to dismiss them from their positions or expel them from the church. It's because he is the one who established the Corinthian church and gave birth to them through the gospel.

Though Paul was ministering at another place at the time, he could still punish them or rebuke them. How is it with you? Do you want to meet the God of love and meekness, or the God of punishment? We shouldn't meet God in a situation where He has to punish us!

Chapter 5

LESSONS ON ADULTERY

— How to Deal with Sexual Immorality

— Get Rid of Old Leaven

— Don't Associate with Immoral People

How to Deal with Sexual Immorality

> It is actually reported that there is immorality among you, and immorality of such a kind as does not exist even among the Gentiles, that someone has his father's wife. You have become arrogant and have not mourned instead, so that the one who had done this deed would be removed from your midst. (5:1-2)

The apostle Paul heard that there was immorality among the believers in Corinth. Immorality refers to sexually immoral, lewd, and indecent acts. What kind of immorality was there in the Corinthian church that Paul said, "...immorality of such a kind as does not exist even among the Gentiles"?

Someone had a sexual relationship with his father's wife. Here, the term 'his father's wife' refers to a step-mother or the woman who was the concubine of the man's father. She is not the biological mother, but she is still, in a sense, a 'mother' for she is the father's wife. Since somebody was maintaining such a relationship with her, Paul said this kind of thing did not exist even among the Gentiles.

We have such an incident in the Old Testament, too. Reuben had such a relation with his father's concubine, Bilhah, and Jacob heard about it (Genesis 35:22). When Jacob was on his deathbed, he called all his twelve sons and said to Reuben, *"Uncontrolled as water, you shall not have preeminence, because you went up to your father's bed; then you defiled it–he went up to my couch"* (Genesis 49:4).

Of course, something like this happens among the Gentiles, too. But Paul said such a thing did not exist even among the Gentiles in order to emphasize that such a thing should not even exist among members of the church.

What if something like this happens in the church? Those who love God and have faith will naturally mourn over the matter. They will pray and fast saying, "God, have mercy on him, and please forgive our church for disgracing You."

But the members of Corinthian church were arrogant and they didn't even have any remorse over it. They didn't do anything about it thinking it had nothing to do with them personally.

Paul said, "You have become arrogant." Arrogance is an attitude of superiority manifested in an overbearing manner in presumptuous claims or assumptions that shows contempt or disregard towards others. Those who have received the Holy Spirit and know the Word of God must not act with arrogance.

What, then, is spiritual arrogance? When we first accept the Lord and are full of the Holy Spirit, we all become humble. New believers, when they are full of the Spirit, are humble to everybody and show their thanks. They understand even those who do not speak to them in a polite and kindly manner. They feel everyone is charming and pleasant.

When people are full of the Holy Spirit in the beginning, they become humble and they would mourn if they were to see something that disgraces God. But when they think they stand on the rock of faith to some extent, some people begin to think they are better than others just because they pray a lot and know the Word of God well.

As they become increasingly arrogant, their actions in accordance with the truth decrease. They do not realize the groaning of the Holy Spirit in them. Even when others disgrace God or commit sins, they do not consider it heart-breaking. When a brother in faith commits sins, they think of it as somebody else's matter. They do not have any concern for him but pass judgment and criticism on him instead. If we have no arrogance we will think of every matter of the church as our own. So, if a brother in faith sins, we will mourn tearing our heart as if we ourselves have committed the sin.

As the members of the Corinthian church became arrogant, they did not mourn over the disgraceful things that were occurring in the church nor did they do anything about it. They were just thinking, "If you fall into destruction with your sins, that is your business. It's enough just for me to live in the truth."

For I, on my part, though absent in body but present in spirit, have already judged him who has so committed this, as though I were present. (5:3)

The apostle Paul says he was "absent in body but present in spirit" with the Corinthian church. Therefore, in spirit he had already judged the man who had taken his father's wife. The actions of the person who had committed such a sin should not be accepted at all. Paul had already judged that the heart of this person was so hardened that it had to be forsaken by God.

Now, the apostle Paul instructed them what to do before they faced the wrath of God. Namely, since the man had such a heart that he would not repent and turn back at all, they had to remove him from the church.

Some may wonder, "If the Bible teaches us not to pass judgment on anybody, why is Paul judging somebody in this case?" Of course, according to the Word of God we must not judge anybody, but there are some people who do have the qualifications to do it.

Matthew 7:5 says, *"You hypocrite, first take the log out of your own eye, and then you will see clearly to take the speck out of your brother's eye."*

Those who have 'removed the planks from their eyes' namely, those who live in the Word of truth completely, are able to clearly see the specks of other brothers correctly. Only those men of spirit who have cast away all forms of evil have the qualifications to judge others. The apostle Paul was such a man.

Therefore, we should not misunderstand this verse and think that we can also judge others as Paul did. Before we judge others, we first have to look back on ourselves completely, cast away all forms of evil, and live in the Word.

Only those men of spirit who are humble, full of love, and able to mourn for others, and who love God to the utmost degree have met the requirements to judge others.

> **In the name of our Lord Jesus, when you are assembled, and I with you in spirit, with the power of our Lord Jesus, *I have decided* to deliver such a one to Satan for the destruction of his flesh, so that his spirit may be saved in the day of the Lord Jesus. (5:4-5)**

The apostle Paul was in a deep spiritual level, and when he was writing these books of the New Testament, he also had endless inspiration of the Holy Spirit. Verses 4 and 5 carry deeply significant meanings together with implied spiritual meanings as well.

We see some passages in the Bible that are difficult to interpret. We cannot understand the proper meaning of such passages unless God explains them to us through the Holy Spirit. Today, many people interpret such words and passages literally. In doing so they think they can be saved even though they consciously commit sins. What, then, is the spiritual meaning contained in verses 4 and 5?

If we interpret this passage literally, we may think, "When we sin for the moment of this life, we will be given over to Satan to go through some kind of trial of retribution. However, when we repent and turn back, only our flesh will be destroyed, and our spirit will still receive salvation when the Lord comes again."

But Revelation 3:5 says, *"He who overcomes will thus be clothed in white garments; and I will not erase his name from the book of life."* The Lord says He will not erase his name from the book of life *if he overcomes.* In other words, if he does not overcome, the Lord will erase his name from the book of life. Moreover, we also understand that the Holy Spirit can be quenched as 1 Thessalonians 5:19 says, *"Do not quench the Spirit."*

From the Bible, we also learn that there are sins that can be forgiven as well as sins that cannot be forgiven. Those who blaspheme or speak and act against the Holy Spirit, or those who taste the grace of Heaven and go back to the world and corruption cannot be saved. God will not give them the spirit of repentance and they cannot be forgiven of their sins (Hebrews Chapters 6 & 10). So, there shouldn't be misunderstanding about our salvation.

Next the apostle Paul says, "when you are assembled, and I with you in spirit, with the power of our Lord Jesus." This means before we decide anything that is related to God, we have to gather in the name of Jesus Christ and decide what to do in His name. Even though our ideas seem to be right, they are wrong if they are not in accordance with God's Word. Only the truth of God is true, and it is only right when we decide something within the truth of God.

Thus, verse 5 means that the apostle Paul and the members of the Corinthian church have gathered in spirit under the name of the Lord Jesus, and by the power of the Lord Jesus they drove out from the church the person who had demonstrated unrepentant immorality. God tells us to love our enemies, so why did they expel him from the church? To have such an immoral relationship with one's father's wife did not exist, even among the Gentiles. So, it could never be accepted in the church.

Someone who doesn't know the Word of God might commit sins. But if somebody who knows the Word of God commits such a sin, he cannot be forgiven, for this kind of a person has the stubbornness of heart which stops him from repenting of his sins. If this kind of a person is present in the church, he will have negative influence on the church members. They may also think that such a person can be also forgiven and commit sins themselves.

When he heard that there was such immorality in the Corinthian church, the apostle Paul understood that the news was correct. The Bible tells us to have two or three witnesses to testify to somebody's sins (Deuteronomy 19:15).

We cannot accuse anybody just by hearing from one witness

because there are false witnesses. We must have at least two or three witnesses.

The apostle Paul, too, did not just listen to one person but confirmed the matter after hearing from a number of people. Only after that did he pass his message to them telling them to remove that sinner from the church for the man would not repent and would not be forgiven.

Then, the members of the Corinthian church had a meeting and sent the person who had committed such immorality out of the church, believing that the will of the apostle Paul was the same as the will of God.

If somebody is lawfully driven out from a church, he will soon be captured by Satan. It's because Matthew 18:18 says, *"Truly I say to you, whatever you bind on earth shall have been bound in heaven; and whatever you loose on earth shall have been loosed in heaven."*

As the church decided to discard the person who committed such an immoral act, he was forsaken by God and given over to Satan.

Of course, it doesn't mean everyone who is driven out of the church is forsaken forever. Suppose somebody has committed a sin, which can be forgiven and from which he can repent and turn back. But the church makes a mistake in decision and removes him. In such a case, God will not forsake him.

God promised us that He will forgive us even 'seventy times seven,' if we repent and turn back (Matthew 18:22). Also, He said in Psalm 103:12, *"As far as the east is from the west, so far has He removed our transgressions from us."*

Therefore, when somebody commits a sin, the church should understand him, forgive him, and pray for him if he can repent and turn away from sins.

Flesh Refers to Sinful Natures

Verse 5 says, *"I have decided to deliver such a one to Satan for the destruction of his flesh, so that his spirit may be saved in the day of the Lord Jesus."* What does this mean? The first part is about the fact that they removed the person who committed immorality, and the latter part is a message for God's children, which is not related to the person who acted immorally.

Therefore, we should not relate the latter half with the first half of the verse. Namely, saying that Paul gave out to Satan the person who had his father's wife means he wanted to save the spirit of the believers of the Corinthian church at the Second Coming of the Lord, even by putting their flesh into death.

When sinful nature, which comes into men through the enemy devil, is combined with the body, the result is referred to as 'flesh'. Paul gave the person who had sexual immorality over to Satan in order to allow for the believers in the church of Corinth to completely cast off sinful natures and receive a 'complete salvation' by becoming complete men of spirit.

Had such a person not been cast out from the church, other believers would have committed similar kinds of sins and eventually they'd have gotten to the point that they would not receive salvation. Thus, in this kind of a case the church should remove such a person so that the other church members might realize that they too could be driven out of the church when they commit such sins.

Get Rid of Old Leaven

**Your boasting is not good. Do you not know that a
little leaven leavens the whole lump *of dough*? (5:6)**

Paul says "Your boasting is not good." Of what did they
boast?

We have seen that the believers in Corinth did not mourn
even when one of them disgraced God greatly with sexual
immorality. Paul said this was something arrogant. But yet,
they prayed to God saying, "God, he committed a sin which
does not exist even among the Gentiles, and so I thank You that
I love You and did not commit such a sin according to Your
Word."

Now, what is the reason that Paul rebuked them saying,
"Your boasting is not good"?

First, it is because we have nothing to boast of on this earth.

Our lives are only transitory and our bodies will go back to a handful of dust after death. James 4:14-16 says, *"Yet you do not know what your life will be like tomorrow. You are just a vapor that appears for a little while and then vanishes away. Instead, you ought to say, 'If the Lord wills, we will live and also do this or that.' But as it is, you boast in your arrogance; all such boasting is evil."*

Even if we do not sin at all and live in the Word of God, we cannot boast of being without sin either. This is possible only by the power of God, not by our own strength.

But the believers in the Corinthian church did not even drive away a person who had immorality but rather they boasted as if they were holy, because they were arrogant. Paul says it was not right because they were boasting seeing God's glory was damaged.

Second, it is because a little leaven leavens the whole lump of dough.

Here, 'leaven' spiritually refers to sins. The Bible writes about many kinds of sins such as hatred, envy, strife, etc. Comparing immorality with a little leaven does not mean that the sin was light. It means the immorality was a part of the many kinds of sins.

'The whole lump' means the whole congregation of the church in Corinth. When Paul said, "Do you not know that a little leaven leavens the whole lump of dough?" he meant that the believers in Corinth were now boasting that they were living in the truth criticizing the person who sinned, but in fact, they would finally receive the works of Satan as well if they accepted that person. That is why Paul said their boasting was not right.

There are some people who cannot keep their heart because of their environment surrounding them.

Those children who see their father drinking everyday and living in pursuit of life's pleasures usually think they won't follow their father's path. Yet in many cases they do the same or even worse after they grow up.

The members in the church of Corinth could also be tempted and commit sins if they accepted the person who sinned. They could have gone into deeper level of sins if they began to think, "If such a grave sin was overlooked, then a little sin must be OK."

Thus, if one person commits sins, we have to take care of that matter quickly. If we leave it alone, just as a little leaven leavens the whole lump, the number of sinners will increase drastically and the whole congregation will be corrupted.

Clean out the old leaven so that you may be a new lump, just as you are *in fact* unleavened. For Christ our Passover also has been sacrificed. (5:7)

The apostle Paul gave advice to the believers in Corinthian church saying they were unleavened, for they had accepted Jesus Christ and were forgiven of their sins. Here, the 'unleavened' means 'God's children who are sinless'.

Even if we accept Jesus Christ and receive the forgiveness of sins, we have to clean out the old leaven to become a completely new person. Here, 'old leaven' refers to all kinds of sins and evil, the thoughts that are against the truth, and bad habits. Paul is saying that we have to clean out these old leavens to become a new person.

Paul continued to say, "For Christ our Passover also has been sacrificed." Passover is the Feast to remember that God saved the sons of Israel when He was pouring down the plague of the deaths of the firstborns of Egypt (Exodus 12:12). The sons of Israel killed a lamb, put its blood on the doorposts and the lintel, and hurriedly ate the meat along with bitter herbs and unleavened bread inside the house to avoid the plague.

The lamb refers to Jesus Christ, and the blood is the precious blood of the Lord. Thus, saying 'For Christ our Passover' means Jesus Christ became the atoning sacrifice to save us.

Jesus Christ sacrificed Himself on the cross to redeem us from sins, and we cannot be saved if we keep on living in sins. This is the reason why they had to drive away the person who willfully committed acts of sexual immorality from the church.

Therefore let us celebrate the feast, not with old leaven, nor with the leaven of malice and wickedness,

but with the unleavened bread of sincerity and truth.
(5:8)

'Feast' here refers to the Passover.

And today, we carry on the spiritual meaning of keeping the Passover by the celebration of Easter. It is the day to celebrate the fact that Jesus shed His blood on the cross and then broke the authority of death through His resurrection. Jesus Christ is the Lord of the Sabbath, and 'feast' here also refers to all Sundays, not just the Easter (Matthew 12:8).

When we observe such feasts, we have to cast away old leaven and wicked heart, and live a sanctified and holy life. Then, we have to worship in spirit and truth (John 4:24).

Malice is the intent to commit an unlawful act or cause harm without legal justification or excuse. Wickedness is something morally very bad, being full of sins. Before we worship God, we first have to look back on ourselves as to whether we have committed any kind of sin. If we have, we have to repent of it first so we will have the proper heart for worship.

Sins of malice are the sins that are not acceptable. We sometimes see those who commit such sins. But if they truly repent and turn back, God will have mercy on them and change them into faithful and truthful persons.

Then, Paul said, "Let us celebrate the feast ... but with the unleavened bread of sincerity and truth." Jesus said, *"I am the bread of life."* And *"I am the living bread that came down out of heaven"* (John 6:48-51).

He explains that we can go the way of eternal life when we offer to God a living sacrifice in spirit and truth, with a pure and truthful heart after cleaning out the old leaven.

Don't Associate with Immoral People

> I wrote you in my letter not to associate with immoral people; I *did* not at all *mean* with the immoral people of this world, or with the covetous and swindlers, or with idolaters, for then you would have to go out of the world. (5:9-10)

Paul wrote the same kind of letter and sent to many other churches, too. He advised other church members not to associate with immoral people. We should understand what kind of attitude churches should show to those who are sexually immoral in the church.

Paul advises the believers in 2 Thessalonians 3:6, *"Now we command you, brethren, in the name of our Lord Jesus Christ, that you keep away from every brother who leads an unruly life and not according to the tradition which you received from us,"* and he continues in Verse 14-15, *"If anyone does not obey our instruction in this letter, take special note of that person and do not associate with him, so that he will be put to shame. Yet do not regard him as an enemy, but admonish him as a brother.''*

All the words written in the letters are the Words of God. So, Paul tells them not to associate with those who disobeyed those words. Then, they would not be put to shame.

If those who are put to shame have just a little bit of faith, they will repent and try to come into the boundary of the brothers in faith again, realizing that the other brothers keep away from them because of their sins.

On the contrary, if they do not have such faith, they will leave the church thinking that there are many other churches. But those who truly believe in God will not act this way.

Therefore, saying "take special note of that person and do not associate with him, so that he will be put to shame," was a way to let the sinners come to repentance, not to hate them. Keep in mind that while the members of the church keep away from them, one of the closest friends should also advise him to turn away from sins.

Now, let us talk about what kinds of sexual immoralities there are.

First, it is physical immorality.

If a married person has a sexual relationship with somebody other than his/her spouse, or if unmarried people have sexual relationships, these acts are 'immoralities'.

These are sins before God. But there may be some married couples who couldn't have the wedding ceremony for various reasons, and we don't say they have sinned for they are recognized as a husband and a wife by others, too. But of course it's better for them to have the wedding ceremony to have official acknowledgment of marriage.

Secondly, there is spiritual adultery.

God gave us life. It is also God who made the semen of men and the egg of women. He gave birth to our spirit, and He is our Father who guides us to the way of eternal life and will dwell with us forever in the kingdom of Heaven.

Therefore it is the duty of God's children to love God first. But if they love something/somebody else more than God, this is spiritual adultery.

For example, if somebody loves his parents, wife, or children, or the worldly fame, social power, knowledge, money, or worldly pleasure more than God, it is spiritual immorality.

Thirdly, there is adultery committed in heart.

Jesus said in Matthew 5:27-28, *"You have heard that it was said, 'You shall not commit adultery'; but I say to you that everyone who looks at a woman with lust for her has already committed adultery with her in his heart."*

In the Old Testament, it was considered a sin only when it was actually committed in action. But in the New Testament, why is it considered a sin even if it is just in the heart?

In the Old Testament times, they had to overcome the sins with only their own strength, and therefore, it was not sin unless it was committed in deed. But in the New Testament times, we can control our heart with the help of the Holy Spirit, and thus, not only our action but also having sinful thoughts in mind is considered sin.

Because the Holy Spirit dwells in us, we can receive the strength from above through our prayers and we can control our heart and cast away sins with that strength. Namely, we can circumcise our heart. This way we can have clean and pure hearts.

In the Old Testament times, they just had to have holy deeds, but in the New Testament times, we have to have the holiness of heart. God says we are still sinful when our heart is unclean, even though we may have holy deeds on the outside.

How can we cast off the adulterous mind?

If we believe in the power of God and pray earnestly, the Holy Spirit will remove our desire to commit adultery in the heart, and eventually we won't feel any kind of heartfelt agitation. The following are the stages to cast off the adulterous mind.

Stage one, it is the level in which, through consistent prayers, we block the adulterous mind that comes to our heart through thoughts.

Even a woman who has a husband may commit adultery in heart when she sees a very handsome man. A man who has a wife may commit adultery in heart when he sees a beautiful woman, a picture of a naked woman, or an adulterous situation.

Even though they don't commit adultery in action, what do they have to do when such thoughts are coming into their mind? They have to believe in the power of God and pray continually and persistently. They will finally be able to block such thoughts if they continue to pray, "God, give me the strength so I won't have adulterous thoughts in mind. Enable me to control and block my thoughts."

Of course, praying is not everything. They have to try not to have such adulterous thoughts. We will finally be able to control our thoughts through the grace of God and the help of the Holy Spirit when we ask for God's strength this way.

Stage two concerns the level in which we are able to exercise control over our heart.

In this level, even if we see an adulterous scene, we don't have any adulterous thoughts in the first place if we make up our mind not to have such thoughts. Since we don't have any adulterous thoughts, we won't have adulterous heart. The adultery in heart comes to us through the thoughts along with feelings. But when we block these, sinful thoughts cannot come to us.

Stage three is the level in which we no longer have any thought of the kind no matter what we see.

In this level, we don't have any agitation of thoughts or mind no matter how adulterous and sensual a scene. Thus, we won't have any adulterous mind. In a crowded subway or buses, we may have some contacts with some others unintentionally. But even in these occasions, we won't have any adulterous mind or thoughts. It is the level in which adultery itself has nothing to do with us.

The fourth stage, it is the level in which we cannot think of such things even if we try to.

In this level, we cannot have any adulterous mind even though we try. We are always full of the Holy Spirit since we don't have any other thoughts of that kind.

Distance yourself from the world

Verse 10 says, "I *did* not at all *mean* with the immoral people of this world, or with the covetous and swindlers, or with idolaters, for then you would have to go out of the world." Paul says they must not keep away from all worldly people who were immoral, covetous and swindlers, or idolaters, just because they did not live by the Word of God.

If they were not to associate with such worldly people, they would have had to depart from this world, which means, there would be only Heaven or Hell. We have to live and work with the worldly people while we are living in this world, so we can also bring them to Christ.

Yet there are times when we should not associate with them, although we are living in this world. Suppose those adulterers, the covetous, swindlers, or idolaters are our colleagues or friends.

We may have friendship with them and talk to them to let them know about God. But if we are about to be stained by their acts of adultery, swindling, or idolatry, we have to keep away from them at those times. This way, we will not follow them doing the unrighteous things.

Suppose your child has some friends who lead him to do unlawful things. Then, you would want your child to keep away from them. By the same token, God tells us not to associate with such people if there is a chance for us to follow their sinful deeds.

What if one of your colleagues or friends asks you to come with him to a lewd or errant place? Would you follow him because he is your friend? Obviously, we should refuse such a request. If you cannot make him turn from sins, you should keep away from him, too.

But if we are able to keep our heart and thoughts while standing on the rock of faith and will not be tempted by anything, then, we don't really have to keep away from such people.

To be covetous is to be greedy. Every action that goes beyond one's place is a covetous act. For example, a person visits his neighbor and sees something good he also wants. Even though he needs to practice strict financial constraint he buys it for himself anyway. Another example is a person who just cannot stop eating although he is already full.

Swindling is to obtain money or property by fraud or deceit. This includes loan-sharking, taking things by force, and trying to gain much after contributing only a little.

Idolatry is to make the images of men, women, animals, or the celestial bodies with wood, stone, metal, gold or silver, and to worship them as god.

Deuteronomy 4:23 says, *"So watch yourselves, that you do not forget the covenant of the LORD your God which He made with you, and make for yourselves a graven image in the form of anything against which the LORD your God has commanded you."* A lifeless idol is nothing and has no power whatsoever. It will result in harm to worship any other god or any other thing than the true God the Creator.

But actually, I wrote to you not to associate with any so—called brother if he is an immoral person, or covetous, or an idolater, or a reviler, or a drunkard, or a swindler—not even to eat with such a one. (5:11)

A 'brother' means a brother in faith. If a Christian is sexually immoral, covetous, an idolater, or a reviler, or a drunkard, God tells us, not even to eat with such a person.

To be covetous is to have inordinate desire for wealth or possessions or for another's possessions. It also refers to a person who has excessive desire for food or other possessions. To revile is to use such a foul and abusive language that one cannot even mention.

Here, "not even to eat with such a one" does not mean we should not even eat or associate with such a person in the church. Then, it means there is no love in the church. This verse means we should not follow their sinful deeds.

I mentioned our relations with unbelievers, and it's the same with brothers in faith. If we have weak faith we should avoid such sinful men, for we might be affected by them and in weakness we might commit sins together with them. But if we stand on the rock of faith, we don't have to avoid them. We can advise them with love for them to come to repentance, or guide them to live in the truth by planting faith in them.

> For what have I to do with judging outsiders? Do you not judge those who are within *the church*? But those who are outside, God judges. Remove the wicked man from among yourselves. (5:12-13)

To judge is to discern a matter that is revealed to be right or wrong according to the truth. It is different in meaning when the Bible tells us not to judge. This means we should not pass judgment about matters that are not clearly revealed. Only God knows the heart of men, and such a judgment will be a standing wall of sin between God and us.

But we can discern whether the worldly people, unbelievers are right or wrong according to the truth. If they are covetous, immoral, idolaters, revilers, drunkards, or swindlers, we understand that they are standing against the truth. But we don't even have to judge them because God will judge them according to His will.

When unbelievers are drunkards, we don't have to tell them, "Why do you drink so much? Stop drinking and live in the truth!" God will judge them, and we don't have to.

But suppose a brother in faith has gone to a fortune-teller. Then we should understand he has become an idolater for he doesn't have faith. He could have prayed to God and received the answer from Him, but he still went to ask the demons. Thus, we cannot say he has faith. We can discern such a case according to the truth.

Remove the Wicked Man

Then, verse 13 says, "Remove the wicked man from among yourselves." In verse 11, it told us not to associate or eat with them, but here, it tells us to remove them.

What will be the consequences if we make concessions for the brothers in faith who are immoral, covetous, idolaters, drunkards, and swindlers? The church cannot give them any title or position, and probably the church members wouldn't feel comfortable associating with them. Thus, they will be naturally left out even in the church.

In this case, it's fortunate if they repent and turn back. But if they complain and commit more sins, their consciences will be seared as well. Finally, no truth can go into them, and as explained in the verse 1, they may commit unacceptable sins such as having a sexual relationship with their father's wife.

Those who have already reached the level of sins from which they cannot turn back have such a hardened heart and they cannot repent. That is why the Bible tells us to remove them from the church. Otherwise, they will become bad leaven and affect the believers.

Matthew 18:15-17 says, *"If your brother sins, go and show him his fault in private; if he listens to you, you have won your brother. But if he does not listen to you, take one or two more with you, so that by the mouth of two or three witnesses every fact may be confirmed. If he refuses to listen to them, tell it to the church; and if he refuses to listen even to the church, let him be to you as a Gentile and a tax collector. Truly I say to you, whatever you bind on earth shall have been bound in heaven; and whatever you loose on earth shall have been loosed in heaven."*

This passage tells us that, when a brother sins, we should not spread knowledge of it to other people, but we should first go to him alone and advise him to live in the Word of God. Luckily if the brother listens and repents, it means we have gained a brother for he will receive salvation.

If he does not listen to the advice, then, we have to take a couple more persons who are higher in spiritual order to advise him. We should let him understand that it is sin and he has to turn back to the way of God, and the two or three people have to be the witnesses. If he still doesn't listen, the church must be made aware.

If he still doesn't listen to even the pastor of the church or somebody who is equivalent, then, we should regard him as though a 'Gentile' or a 'tax-collector'. In this context a gentile is one who does not believe in God, and the tax-collectors were considered sinners. So this has the intended meaning that we should regard him as a worldly unbeliever or a sinner.

Verse 18 says, "Whatever you bind on earth shall have been bound in heaven; and whatever you loose on earth shall have been loosed in heaven." When a representative of the church advises him, if he turns away, then God will acknowledge him, too. Otherwise, he will be given out to Satan. Therefore, the representatives of the church must have the love to endure with him and pray for him until the end.

But this verse cannot be applied to new believers who have just accepted the Lord. Those who recently began to attend church don't really understand the Word of God. They don't even know what sin is. Even though they do, they lack the strength and power to practice the Word.

So, we should not think we have to avoid them for they are still sinning, but rather we should plant faith in them and let them come into the truth more and more.

But when those who have faith and even some positions in the church commit such grave sins, we should not associate with them.

Chapter 6

LAWSUITS AMONG BELIEVERS

— Problems among the Church Members

— Saints Will Judge the World

— To Their Shame

— Sins Leading to Death

— What Should We Live For?

— Spiritual Meaning of Prostitute

Problems among the Church Members

> Does any one of you, when he has a case against his
> neighbor, dare to go to law before the unrighteous and
> not before the saints? (6:1)

In chapter 6, Paul writes about the will of God concerning
lawsuits among the brothers in faith and he explains the ways to
solve the problems that arise in the church.

We may become an 'unrighteous person' like that mentioned
by Paul and not receive salvation if we do not properly
understand the will of God with regard to lawsuits. Some may
think they won't become involved in such a situation in the
church in the first place for they are faithful Christians.

However, we should still be able to give proper answers in
accordance with the truth when new believers or other brothers
in faith seek counsel through us concerning lawsuits.

In verse 1 of chapter 6 we can see that there was a lawsuit

filed between church members in the church of Corinth. A believer was suing another brother in faith over a legal matter before the unrighteous.

The term 'unrighteous' refers to worldly people who do not know the truth and do not live in the Word of God. We can also say church members who doubt the Word of God and do not live by it are 'unrighteous'.

So, if we go to such a person in the church with a problem, it is same as going to an unrighteous unbeliever to solve a problem. It is not the right thing to do. It is not appropriate for us to sue a brother in faith in the courts of the world, either.

The functioning of the law of the world cannot operate in the same way as the law of God written in the Bible. God tells us to love our enemies, consider others better than ourselves, and understand and forgive others. It also tells us that we will be 'lifted when we serve' and we will 'win when we lose.'

Only the Word of God is the never-changing truth, and we can live a happy life only if we follow it. But many people refuse to live by the Word of God and they follow their own interests.

Furthermore the law of the world and the law of God are not the same. Therefore, how foolish it is for believers to rely on the laws of the world and not rely solely on the law of God?

That is why the apostle Paul rebuked the believers in the Corinthian church for they did not try to solve the problem within the church among the brothers in faith but went to the unrighteous people who did not know the truth.

Saints Will Judge the World

> Or do you not know that the saints will judge the
> world? If the world is judged by you, are you not
> competent *to constitute* the smallest law courts? (6:2)

It says the saints will judge the world. Who are saints then?
When somebody registers in a church, we say he is a church
member. Of the church members, those who keep the Word of
God in their hearts, make spiritual food of it and practice it in
their lives are called the saints.

Why are these people called 'saints'? Doesn't that refer to
those who led lives of exceptional holiness?

John 14:6 says, *"Jesus said to him, 'I am the way, and the
truth, and the life; no one comes to the Father but through
Me.'"* Only the Word of God is the truth, which is eternally
never changing. Therefore, God's Word will be realized in
actuality for those who believe the promise of God in the Bible

and follow His Word.

If God is not alive, the Bible is also dead, and it cannot be the truth. But God lives. He existed before eternity and exists throughout all eternity. He never changes and His Word is the absolute truth. Also, Jesus Christ is His one and only Son who came to this earth. He is also the Word and the truth itself.

The Word of God, which is the truth, is holy, and thus we call those who follow it 'saints.' On the other hand, those who only attend church are called 'churchgoers.'

Of course, we can also call them 'new believers' or 'new comers.' The reason why we come to church and register as church members is to become God's children and receive salvation. We do it to listen to the Word of God and follow the holy path. So, it is completely appropriate to call the new believers 'saints.'

There are some people who are standing on the rock of faith. There are others who are trying hard to live by the Word of God but they are not yet standing on the rock of faith.

Paul said, "Or do you not know that the saints will judge the world?" Here 'the saints' refers to the children of God who stand on the rock of faith. These saints have the ability to judge the world. As explained above, when there are problems in the world, they can discern whether a certain thing is right or wrong, or whether it is true or false according to the truth.

That is why Paul is asking how come they couldn't take care of the problem between brothers in faith, when the saints can judge the matters of this world. Those who stand on the rock of faith have the ability to solve the problems that arise among the brothers in faith, and therefore believers have no reason to go to the world for lawsuits of the world.

Do you not know that we will judge angels? How much more matters of this life? (6:3)

Verse 3 is the supplement to the verse 2. We understand about the angels through the Bible. To judge angels doesn't mean we will pass judgment on them with an evil mind but to discern the things according to the truth.

For example, from the Bible in 2 Peter 2:4, we understand that God did not spare angels when they sinned, but He cast them into Hell and committed them to 'pits of darkness,' that are reserved for judgment.

Also, Jude 1:6 says, *"And angels who did not keep their own domain, but abandoned their proper abode, He has kept in eternal bonds under darkness for the judgment of the great day."*

The Bible writes about angels who bring down rain, move the clouds, mighty angels, and powerful angels as in 2 Peter 2:11 which mentions angels who are 'greater in might and power'.

Luke 1:19 talks about Gabriel, saying, *"The angel answered and said to him, 'I am Gabriel, who stands in the presence of God, and I have been sent to speak to you and to bring you this good news.'"* It was the scene in which Gabriel appeared to deliver the news of the birth of John the Baptist.

Moreover Daniel 10:13 says, *"But the prince of the kingdom of Persia was withstanding me for twenty-one days; then behold, Michael, one of the chief princes, came to help me, for I had been left there with the kings of Persia."* We have a record about Michael the archangel. We can discern about the angels in spiritual realm through the Bible, though they are not seen with our eyes.

So, by saying, "Do you not know that we will judge angels? How much more matters of this life?" Paul emphasizes that we can judge the matters of this world for we can judge the spiritual beings like angels.

So if you have courts of law dealing with matters of this life, do you appoint them as judges who are of no account in the church? (6:4)

There may be some problems among the believers because of the matters of this world. So, if something like this happens in the church what should we do if two people have a quarrel or problem and are not able to settle it within the church?

The saints who stand on the rock of faith can discern between what is right and wrong with the Word of God, and so, we should let them resolve the situation. But they didn't do so in the Corinthian church. That is why Paul pointed out that they appointed as judges those who were of no account in the church.

If a dispute arises among the brothers in faith due to matters of the world and they sue each other, their acts are those of unrighteous people who do not live in the truth.

For example, suppose a person who is not living in the truth is slandering and criticizing another person in the church. Further suppose someone else heard it and joined him. When a couple of people join with such a person, a group is created.

When something happens to a person who belongs to such a group, he will naturally go to his unrighteous friends to ask them what he should do. Now, when the unrighteous people advise him, will it be appropriate? Will it be the right way to resolve the problem? Chances are that it will not be! Those who are unrighteous cannot give an answer within the truth because they themselves are not living in the truth. That is why Paul asked, "...do you appoint them as judges who are of no account in the church," pointing out that it was not right thing to do.

To Their Shame

I say *this* to your shame. *Is it* so, that there is not among you one wise man who will be able to decide between his brethren, but brother goes to law with brother, and that before unbelievers? (6:5-6)

The apostle Paul said in 1 Corinthians 4:14, *"I do not write these things to shame you, but to admonish you as my beloved children."* But here, he said, "I say this to your shame." It's because the situation now is completely different from that of the chapter 4 of 1 Corinthians.

In 1 Corinthians chapter 4, we see that when the apostles were reviled, they accepted it as blessing; when they were persecuted, they endured; when they were slandered, they tried to conciliate. This is the right way, and the believers in the church of Corinth should have done the same. But they didn't.

Paul didn't want to boast of himself or put the Corinthian

believers to shame. He just wanted to teach them with the heart of the parents that the deeds of the apostles were right.

But in Verse 5, Paul says, "I say *this* to your shame." He made it clear that he was not going to say something good to his beloved children. He meant he had to say it to their shame to point out their wrongdoings. Though they may have felt the shame, for Paul to say this was to let them bear it in their minds so they wouldn't ever act in the same way again.

God's children must not sue each other. But in the Corinthian church, the brothers in faith were quick to sue and sued each other before the unbelievers. That is why Paul had to say it was to their shame.

How to Solve Problems in the Lord

Now, what should we do if we have a worldly matter with another brother in faith? We should follow the order of the church to deal with it. If you are a lay believer you should first consult your cell leader. If he/she cannot solve the problem, you should go up in the order of the church.

Finally, you can go up to the pastor of the church. If the problem is still not solved, you should go to the church council, or a meeting or organization that can represent the whole church to discern what is right or wrong.

In most cases such matters are about money. I have been advising the church members not to have any kind of money exchange whatsoever in the church. Many misunderstandings and problems are caused because of money.

If you must borrow some money due to an emergency, you should not borrow from any brother in faith but from somebody outside the church. It is to disobey the Word of God to have exchange of money among the brothers in faith, so Satan will cause strife and problems.

I have seen many church members have difficulties because of lending and borrowing money among the church members.

Some people cannot just refuse when another person asks them to lend them some money. So, they borrow from a third party or place to lend the money to that person. But many people do not pay it back within the promised time. Romans 13:8 says, *"Owe nothing to anyone except to love one another."* As said, we should never lay a burden on a brother in faith because of money.

Actually, then, it is already a defeat for you, that you have lawsuits with one another. Why not rather be wronged? Why not rather be defrauded? On the contrary, you yourselves wrong and defraud. *You do* this even to *your* brethren. (6:7-8)

If a brother in faith sues another brother in faith, it proves that this person is an unrighteous man who does not live in the truth, not a child of God. It reveals he is a false believer, even though he might have seemed to have devout faith, working faithfully in the church.

Then, what should you do if another brother in faith sues you? If you have true faith, you will be willing to take up the loss that is caused by it, rather than fighting against the person to reveal whose fault it is. That is why the apostle Paul advises in verse 7 to be wronged and defrauded rather than to quarrel and become an evil person.

But those new believers who do not know the truth very well are apt to think it is right to reveal who is innocent by fighting back according to justice.

Even if we are wronged and defrauded, it is not really a loss. Satan will certainly lose and the righteousness will win only if we live in the truth. God dwells in righteousness and searches the heart of men. Thus, it may seem that you are facing a loss for the moment, but God will surely work for the good of everything at the proper time.

This way, there must not be any lawsuits among the brothers in faith, but the members of the Corinthian church acted in unrighteousness, revealing the evil that existed among themselves. Unrighteous people were in the church pretending to be the children of God and to live in the truth. But later it was disclosed that they were not children of God nor did they live in the truth. After all, they cheated one another.

This kind of unrighteous thing should not happen in a church. Even among the unbelievers, if they sue a member of their own family, people would say it is evil. And how can it be accepted when there are lawsuits among the brothers in faith who believe in God? If this kind of a thing happens, it is sure that person is unrighteous.

James 1:22 says, *"But prove yourselves doers of the word, and not merely hearers who delude themselves."* As said, if you just hear but do not practice the Word, you are a liar and a cheater of yourself. If the believers in Corinth really believed in God, they wouldn't sue each other.

Verse 8 says, "On the contrary, you yourselves wrong and defraud. *You do* this even to your brethren." This means that it is an act of unrighteousness to sue another brother, and they say they believed in God even after suing their brother. Therefore they were cheating themselves.

God tells us to love even our enemies. He has let us receive salvation by sacrificing His one and only Son Jesus on the cross. We who have received this grace for free can never sue any brother in faith.

Sins Leading to Death

> Or do you not know that the unrighteous will not inherit the kingdom of God? Do not be deceived; neither fornicators, nor idolaters, nor adulterers, nor effeminate, nor homosexuals, nor thieves, nor the covetous, nor drunkards, nor revilers, nor swindlers, will inherit the kingdom of God. (6:9-10)

Even among the believers, those who are unrighteous will not inherit the kingdom of God. It means they will not be saved. God's Word is given to the believers. Unbelievers have nothing to do with the Word of God in the first place.

So, the 'unrighteous' here refers to those who say they are believers, but do not live according to the Word of God. They will not be saved.

Jesus said, in Matthew 7:21, *"Not everyone who says to Me, 'Lord, Lord,' will enter the kingdom of heaven, but he who does the will of My Father who is in heaven will enter."* Also, even though we might act like prophets, manifest powerful works, and drive out demons, the Lord will say He doesn't know us if we live in lawlessness.

We cannot be saved just by saying we believe in the Lord, keeping the Lord's Day, giving the tithes and helping the needy, but by living according to the Word of God. Even if we do many things for God, Jesus will say, "I never knew you," if we practice lawlessness (Matthew 7:23).

We may be deceived if we do not understand this very clearly. It's not only unbelievers who deceive us. We can be deceived by people who say they believe, but practice unrighteousness by not living in the Word of God.

Some believers say that we don't have to be extremists in faith. They urge us to just attend Sunday morning service and go fishing, mountain climbing or a picnic in the afternoon. They say some elders of a church also drink alcohol, and so it is OK to drink a couple of glasses. But God tells us not to be deceived by such words.

What is unrighteousness then? Verse 8 says that it is unrighteousness to sue a brother in faith. Moreover, unrighteousness is everything that is against the truth and every act that is not according to the Word of God.

Verses 9 and 10 mention some of the things that are unrighteous.

Fornication is sexual conduct that is unclean and lewd. Idolatry is not only worshipping images of gold, silver, stones, or metal, but also loving something or someone more than God. Adultery is having a sexual relationship between men and women who are not lawfully acknowledged by God to be attached to each other.

An effeminate is considered a man whose behavior, appearance or speech is excessively characteristic of a woman or girl. They are mostly found outside the church, but there are some in the church, too. For example, some men like the company of women and behave like a woman to an unusual extent.

Homosexuals are not forgiven by God and these people cannot receive salvation. When those who have been homosexuals before they come to believe in the Lord, they must now repent and turn back so they can be forgiven. But if they still do not turn back and just keep on doing the same thing, it means they cannot receive salvation.

Thieves have many meanings but generally, it is to steal somebody else's possessions with heart or action. Judas Iscariot was a thief, too. He stole the money saying he was helping the poor.

Next, we have the covetous and drunkards. God is not

delighted with getting drunk. Alcohol cannot give us any benefit. It is for pleasure that people make alcoholic drinks. It's not meant to be a healthy drink. If we live in Jesus Christ and in the truth, we should naturally quit drinking.

The Bible teaches us not to get drunk (Ephesians 5:18). When alcohol goes into our body, we lose the control over our body and mind, and we will do the things that are against the truth. Some say it is OK to drink a little bit because the Bible only tells us not to get drunk.

But if you drink just a cup, you get drunk that much. The alcohol will go into all parts of your body. If you drink a little, you get drunk a little, and if you drink a lot, you get drunk a lot. Thus we should not say a couple of glasses are OK.

Revilers and swindlers are explained in chapter 5 verse 11. Revilers speak foul language and swindlers take somebody else's money or possessions by deceit. These kinds of persons will not inherit the kingdom of God, which means they will not go into the kingdom of Heaven.

So, if you are still practicing these unrighteous things, you should quickly confess your sins and turn back. God is faithful and righteous to forgive us our sins and to cleanse us from all unrighteousness (1 John 1:9). But if we keep on sinning even after confessing our sins and saying that we will not sin again, it is to mock God. It means we are still dwelling in sins and we cannot be saved this way.

Such were some of you; but you were washed, but you were sanctified, but you were justified in the name of the Lord Jesus Christ and in the Spirit of our God. (6:11)

Many of us were such unrighteous people, but now we have received the Holy Spirit in Jesus Christ. The Holy Spirit lets us realize what sin is and gives us faith.

When we repent and turn away, the blood of the Lord cleanses us. Though we have sinned before, if we repent and turn back, God cleanses us through the blood of the Lord Jesus who was crucified. This way, we will reach salvation.

But if we just say we believe in God while committing acts of unrighteousness, God does not acknowledge it as faith, and we cannot be saved. God considers it faith and saves us when we try to live according to the Word of God and struggle against sins to cast them away. God will say we are righteous when we become more and more sanctified through this process and effort of struggling against sins.

All things are lawful for me, but not all things are profitable. All things are lawful for me, but I will not be mastered by anything. (6:12)

"All things are lawful for me" means we have the freedom to choose to live in the truth or in the unrighteousness. All depends on our choices. But not all of our choices are profitable. Only to live in Jesus Christ is profitable.

In order to inherit the kingdom of Heaven, we have to live in the truth completely not being mastered by anything. We have to boldly follow the will of God. If we have this kind of faith, we won't be shaken even when our parents or bosses in the work try to stop us from living in the truth.

Once, a believer came to me asking to pray for her. But I remembered that she had once been healed of her illness in our church and given her testimony.

"Pastor, please pray for me. I cannot move my body or use my hands due to palsy."

"Sister, you didn't keep the Lord's Day, did you? Since you received the grace of God, you should have! Why didn't you?"

"I went to work on Sundays because I was afraid of my husband."

She heard of the news of the powerful works of God and came to our church, and was healed of her sickness. But she later compromised with the world in fear of her husband's persecutions.

Jesus said in Matthew 10:28, *"Do not fear those who kill the body but are unable to kill the soul; but rather fear Him who is able to destroy both soul and body in hell."* If we really have faith, we will not profane the Lord's Day, which is commanded by God, even though we might be persecuted or beaten.

God causes all things to work together for good when we believe God is with us and pray. God will lead to salvation even those persecuting parents or husbands. If we keep our faith without compromising, there may be persecutions from family members for the moment, but finally we will be able to evangelize the family.

We may even go away from salvation if we compromise with fear of persecutions. Therefore, we have to boldly follow the will of God and act according to the truth, not fearing any drawbacks.

What Should We Live For?

Food is for the stomach and the stomach is for food, but God will do away with both of them. Yet the body is not for immorality, but for the Lord, and the Lord is for the body. Now God has not only raised the Lord, but will also raise us up through His power. Do you not know that your bodies are members of Christ? Shall I then take away the members of Christ and make them members of a prostitute? May it never be! (6:13-15)

Food is a necessity for life. We can keep our life only when we eat food and get the nutrients. But food will perish after all. When God calls our spirit, our bodies will also perish.

Everything will perish this way. So what should we be living for? Knowing that we won't be able to inherit the kingdom of God if we do not cast away unrighteousness such as immorality, idolatry, adultery, effeminateness, homosexuality, stealing, coveting, getting drunk, reviling, and swindling, how can we live in unrighteousness?

Now, what does it mean by "Yet the body is not for immorality, but for the Lord, and the Lord is for the body"? Jesus died on the cross to lead us into the kingdom of Heaven, because He is for our body. That is why we can inherit the kingdom of Heaven.

We cannot escape falling into Hell if we keep on living in unrighteousness as sinners. Therefore, it is very obvious that we are to live for the Lord who deals with our spirit and leads us to the kingdom of Heaven with the power of God.

Verse 14 says, "Now God has not only raised the Lord, but will also raise us up through His power." He will give us a perfected resurrected body that will not perish.

Verse 15 says, "Do you not know that your bodies are members of Christ? Shall I then take away the members of Christ and make them members of a prostitute? May it never be!" Jesus said, *"I am the vine, you are the branches"* (John 15:5). We are branches that stick to the vine, and so we are one with the vine. We are one with the Lord, and we are all parts of His body.

How holy is the body of the Lord? It is spotless and blameless. Then, the parts of this holy body should also be holy. There are many branches on a tree. If one of the branches becomes sick, we have to cut it off so the whole tree can be healthy. Much in the same way, if one of our arms is decaying, we cannot just leave it, and we have to amputate it.

Or, what if a part of our body becomes dirty right after taking a bath? We cannot just go to bed saying it is OK because all other parts are clean. We will definitely wash it off.

Therefore, God's children, who are parts of the body of the Lord who is spotless and blameless, always have to lead a holy life. If they become unclean, they should wash themselves right away.

Spiritual Meaning of Prostitute

Or do you not know that the one who joins himself to a prostitute is one body with her? For He says, "The two shall become one flesh." But the one who joins himself to the Lord is one spirit with Him. Flee immorality. Every other sin that a man commits is outside the body, but the immoral man sins against his own body. (6:16-18)

Before, the apostle Paul warned the members of the Corinthian church, who are parts of the body of the Christ, not to make themselves the body of a prostitute. Here, 'prostitute' refers to all kinds of unrighteousness mentioned so far.

Fornication, idolatry, adultery, effeminateness, homosexuality, stealing, coveting, getting drunk, reviling, and swindling all belong to the meaning of the term 'prostitute'. We cannot make the body of the Christ a body of a prostitute, namely an unclean body of unrighteousness.

Our Lord has holy and clean body. Thus, we cannot disgrace the Lord becoming a dirty body. It is to disgrace God as well by giving out foul smell, not the fragrance of Christ.

We are not unrighteous people. We are God's children who are cleansed by the precious blood of the Lord. Therefore, we cannot act in unrighteousness; and if we do have unrighteousness in us, we have to cast it away quickly.

Romans 1:18 says, *"For the wrath of God is revealed from heaven against all ungodliness and unrighteousness of men who suppress the truth in unrighteousness."* Also, Colossians 3:25 says, *"For he who does wrong will receive the consequences of the wrong which he has done, and that without partiality."*

God does not look at the appearances but the heart. Having a godly appearance outwardly has no value if we are full of unrighteousness inside. God does not take men by appearance, and so, our hearts should change. We should act in a godly manner not just on the outside; we have to wash our heart with the blood of the Lord everyday to become a holy and righteous child of God.

It is not easy for a man to understand the spiritual meanings in God. Verses 16 and 17 explain the spiritual meaning with a parable to make it easier for men to understand it. A man leaves his parents to become one body with a woman (Genesis 2:24), and in the same way those who unite with a prostitute will become one body with her.

This spiritually means they had to be one body with Jesus our bridegroom, but they didn't. Jesus, our bridegroom, is the truth. We have to become one with the Word of God, but if we follow the untruth, we will be one body with the prostitute.

As already explained, prostitute refers to all kinds of unrighteousness that is against the truth. If we take a prostitute, we become one with her, and in the same way, befriending the world, not living by the Word of God, is 'prostitute' and a man who unites with a prostitute. If we make ourselves unclean by becoming one with a prostitute, we cannot be saved.

But those who are united with our Lord will become one spirit with the Lord. The Holy Spirit lets us realize the Word of God and believe it, and points out our sins to cast them away.

As we live in the truth more and more, we give birth to spirit through the Holy Spirit. We become a complete man of spirit when we cast away untruths and live in the truth completely. At this state, we have the heart of Jesus Christ (Philippians 2:5), and the spirit of the Lord becomes one with our spirit.

Verse 18 says, "Flee immorality. Every other sin that a man commits is outside the body, but the immoral man sins against his own body."

There are two kinds of immorality. The physical meaning is sexual immorality, but we should also understand the spiritual meaning.

God sometimes is depicted as the bride of His people.

And in the Old Testament, those who do not keep the

commandments of God but worship idols or commit sins are referred to as adulteresses. Namely, it is to have immorality if we do not dwell in the Word of God.

Now, what does it mean by "Every other sin that a man commits is outside the body"?

When we cast off sins, we are not connected with sins for the sins are out of our body. We gain freedom from sins, the freedom of truth. We are connected to sins because we have them in us. If we cast them away and dwell in the light and truth, we have nothing to do with sins.

Suppose you don't have any desire to hate or kill anybody. Then, such sins have nothing to do with you; they are out of your body. But those who have immorality, namely, those who compromise with the world and commit unrighteousness, combine themselves with the sins that were out of their body. They now have become one body with unrighteousness.

Or do you not know that your body is a temple of the Holy Spirit who is in you, whom you have from God, and that you are not your own? For you have been bought with a price: therefore glorify God in your body. (6:19-20)

Who gave us our body? It is God the Creator. In the Old Testament times the Holy Spirit did not dwell in men's heart, but He just inspired them from outside to give them prophecies. Thus, people could not keep communication with God continuously. After the inspiration was finished, they had to live only by their own willpower. But in the New Testament times, we can communicate with God all the time because the Holy Spirit has come into our heart.

It means our body has become the sanctuary where the Holy Spirit dwells. How glorious and precious! Since the Holy Spirit dwells in us, we must not become one with a prostitute, namely with unrighteousness. The Holy Spirit is so pure and holy, and how much would He groan if He has to dwell in such a dirty and filthy place!

We may sometimes commit sins while we are living in the truth. Then, we will have the difficult and some kind of uncomfortable feelings in us. It is because the Holy Spirit is groaning in us for He has to dwell in filth. What do we have to do in this case? We have to repent and turn back quickly to please the Holy Spirit.

The passage continues to say, "you are not your own." Before, we used to live as we wanted, living in sins and doing unrighteousness. But we have become the Lord's by the price of His blood. Because He has bought us with His blood, we are not within our own discretion any more.

We have to live by the will of God and the Lord. We have to struggle against sins to live a holy life. Since our bodies are no longer our own, we must not use our bodies as if it were our own.

Our Lord bought us by shedding His pure and precious blood. He gave us His grace and an eternal life with such a price that cannot be exchanged for anything else in this world. Therefore, we have to give glory to God with our body.

We should glorify God and give out the fragrance of Christ even to make many unbelievers say, "I want to attend church when I see you." This is the duty of the believers in God.

1 Corinthians 10:31 says, *"Whether, then, you eat or drink or whatever you do, do all to the glory of God."* Romans 14:7-9 says, *"For not one of us lives for himself, and not one dies for himself; for if we live, we live for the Lord, or if we die, we die for the Lord; therefore whether we live or die, we are the Lord's. For to this end Christ died and lived again, that He might be Lord both of the dead and of the living."*

If we truly believe, we have to cast away unrighteousness and become one with the Lord in the truth. We have to live to the glory of God in whatever we eat, drink, and whatever we do.

Chapter 7

MARRIAGE

Desirable Marriage Life

Now concerning the things about which you wrote, it is good for a man not to touch a woman. But because of immoralities, each man is to have his own wife, and each woman is to have her own husband. The husband must fulfill his duty to his wife, and likewise also the wife to her husband. The wife does not have authority over her own body, but the husband does; and likewise also the husband does not have authority over his own body, but the wife does. (7:1-4)

Paul said that it was good for a man not to touch a woman. He wanted to prevent any kind of test in the church.

A man not touching a woman means that it is better for us to live for God preparing ourselves as brides of the Lord in these last days, since Jesus came to this earth. But if we are to enter into immoralities by not getting married, it is then better to get married.

Suppose we don't get married for the sake of God's work, but then commit acts of sexual immorality and become forsaken by God. How pitiful such a situation would be! If this is the case, it is better to get married and avoid immorality.

Verse 3 says that the husband and the wife have to fulfill their respective duties to each other. Now, what does it mean 'to fulfill one's duty'? The husband has to lead the family in the truth. Also, he has to be strong and courageous like Joshua when God spoke to him (Joshua 1:6-9). A man has to have the attributes that make him a man together with diligence and strong work ethics.

To be strong and courageous doesn't mean he has to become violent. He should be able to accept and embrace others and fulfill his duty to his wife and family with meekness.

What is wife's duty, then? A wife should not boast or raise her voice but be obedient and calm, enduring in all things. She also has to teach her children in the truth.

Are We to Have No Authority over Our Own Bodies?

Now, what does it mean by not having authority over one's own body?

A married couple is not just an individual; they are one body. The husband cannot exercise full control over his own body, and neither can the wife. They should be united as one heart, discussing all matters in peace.

Genesis 2:24 says, *"For this reason a man shall leave his father and his mother, and be joined to his wife; and they shall become one flesh."* Because they are one flesh, they cannot just insist on their own opinions.

When the husband grieves, the wife should also grieve together with him. When the wife rejoices, the husband should also rejoice together with her. They should be one in heart and mind.

In position of authority, the man is above the woman in marriage. But, each of them should acknowledge the authority of the other. The husband won't insist his opinions alone if he acknowledges the authority of the wife, too.

Spiritual Meaning of 'Depriving'

Stop depriving one another, except by agreement for a time, so that you may devote yourselves to prayer, and come together again so that Satan will not tempt you because of your lack of self-control. But this I say by way of concession, not of command. (7:5-6)

It says "Stop depriving one another" and we have to understand it spiritually. It is talking about our hearts.

It means the husband and wife should not be divided in their hearts but become one heart in the truth. It's difficult to have one thought, but it is possible to have one heart. Believers live in the truth, and because there is but one truth, in that truth we can have one heart.

It continues to say, "...except by agreement for a time, so that you may devote yourselves to prayer, and come together again..." If they are not united as one heart, Satan will tempt them. They may feel lonely or troublesome when they are not united as one, and Satan may tempt them in this situation. They may even commit a sin, and thus, they have to be as one in heart again as soon as possible.

But sometimes they may not be able to be physically together. They may have to be separated from each other to accomplish the ministry of God, business, work, or personal situations.

Namely, if one has to fast, retreat to the mountains for prayer, or offer a 100-night long prayer to God, they have to be 'deprived' of one another. They have to do it for a good purpose. But after their prayer is over, they have to come together again.

There is one thing we have to be careful of in this sense of depriving one another. Suppose we want to go to church and pray all night. Then, before we do that, we have to have the agreement of the spouse. If the husband or the wife does not respect the other's opinion but just acts as he/she wants, it may give a rise to quarrels. This means the peace is broken and God is not pleased with it. Their children may go astray, too. Therefore, the husband and wife have to be at peace in all things.

This has both physical as well as spiritual meaning, but actually the meanings are the same. Jesus is our bridegroom and we are His brides. So, we have to be united with our Lord Jesus who is the truth itself. This in turn means that by being united with Christ we will be united and have one heart with God as well. Philippians 2:5 says, *"Have this attitude in yourselves which was also in Christ Jesus."* In order to do this, we have to dwell in the truth. When we dwell in the truth, we are one with Jesus Christ because His heart is the truth itself.

Now, what if we are depriving ourselves of God? Obviously, Satan will tempt us. If we are not united with the truth, it means we look at the world, we are tempted to commit sins, and we will be mocked by Satan in our suffering from the tests and trials that follow sin. But if we have one heart with the Lord in truth, it means we are living by the will of God completely, and thus, we will not face any tests or trials. Even if we do, God will work for the good of everything.

Verse 6 says, "But this I say by way of concession, not of command." The apostle Paul was a very active and strong young man before he accepted the Lord. But from the time he met the Lord, he always rejoiced, gave thanks to the Lord, and changed into a holy person who resembled the Lord.

As he was full of generosity and love, he did not command others to do this or do that when he taught them. Though he was an apostle, he did not demand of the flock, but just taught them and advised them with the Word of God. If we are leaders in the church, we should not be commanding in leadership, but lead by example, concession, and encouragement.

There are times when the whole congregation of the church has to fast and pray for something concerning the kingdom of

God. But even in these occasions, I just say, "We are going to do this in accordance with the will of God. If you are willing and able, you may participate. But, you should decide within your freewill according to the works of the Holy Spirit."

But sometimes, I see some leaders become commanding in their leadership. I am heartbroken to see such a thing and I advise them saying, "Jesus came not to be served but to serve. We have to consider ourselves to be lesser than others."

Not only in the church, but in the family relationships between parents and children, and in society in the relationships between those in leadership positions and those who are subordinate to them, in all relationships, we should have this humbleness like that of the apostle Paul that is the heart of the Lord. It is the heart that guides and leads others with love and generosity and not with orders and commands.

"I Wish that All Men Were Even as I Myself Am"

Yet I wish that all men were even as I myself am. However, each man has his own gift from God, one in this manner, and another in that. (7:7)

The apostle Paul spoke according to the clear voice, inspiration, and guidance of the Holy Spirit. Therefore, what he said was the Word of God.

He said, "I wish that all men were even as I myself am." Then, why did he not say he wanted all men to be as Jesus or God, but like himself?

He had the heart of the Lord by loving God thoroughly and acting in the truth. He wanted everyone to take after all these things. What else should we learn from him? Paul did not marry. He was unmarried in all three of his mission trips.

In 1 Corinthians 9:5-12 Paul is recorded to have said that he had a right to take along a believing wife, even as the rest of the apostles and the brothers of the Lord, and Cephas. But, he didn't do it for the sake of the gospel. He also said he wanted all men to be "as he was."

However, verse 7 says that each man has his own 'gift from God'. This does not refer to such gifts as gift of other tongue, prophecy, or healing. It refers to the grace that they received from God.

We all have received some kind of grace from God. Above all, we were saved from falling into the destruction of Hell. We have also received eternal life. We were changed from children of the devil to the children of God, and our names are recorded in the book of life in Heaven. And, this is just part of the great grace we have received!

But, the level of feeling that grace is different from person to person. Some can say they just want to dedicate their lives solely to God. They do not get married because the grace they received from God is so great.

If I had accepted the Lord and known the truth before getting married, I would have lived like the apostle Paul, too. The grace that God gave me was so great that I wanted to repay Him for His grace with all my heart, mind, soul, strength and life in being faithful to Him. If the grace once received from God is that great, it is good for a man to remain single like the apostle Paul.

But I say to the unmarried and to widows that it is

good for them if they remain even as I. But if they do not have self-control, let them marry; for it is better to marry than to burn *with passion*. (7:8-9)

Paul says to the unmarried and widows that it is good for them to remain as they are like Paul himself. What is the reason?

If they get married they have to take care of their spouse and at the same time serve God, too. Then their mind is divided. The husband may not like it when his wife goes to pray. He just wants her to stay with him. There are some people who are very diligent in the works of God before getting married, but after marriage, they are busy raising their children and taking care of their family matters and become lazy in their works of God. That is why Paul said it is good to remain single.

But he also says we should marry if we do not have self-control. When we see other people getting married and starting a family, if we feel we want to do the same, then, it is better for us to get married.

In Matthew 5:28 Jesus said, *"But I say to you that everyone who looks at a woman with lust for her has already committed adultery with her in his heart."* It is better to get married and have a good, God-serving family rather than being single and committing adultery. It is not a sin to get married and God would not say it is disappointing Him.

Divorce

But to the married I give instructions, not I, but the Lord, that the wife should not leave her husband (but if she does leave, she must remain unmarried, or else be reconciled to her husband), and that the husband should not divorce his wife. But to the rest I say, not the Lord, that if any brother has a wife who is an unbeliever, and she consents to live with him, he must not divorce her. And a woman who has an unbelieving husband and he consents to live with her, she must not send her husband away. (7:10-13)

In verse 6 Paul said it is by way of concession, but here why does he say it is an instruction? When you deliver the Word of God, it is instruction. If you speak your own opinion, it is by way of concession. We have to understand the difference between the way of concession and instruction.

He says it is instruction here because it is not Paul's personal opinion but he is delivering the will of God. When a servant of God delivers the will of God, he cannot say, "It's better to do this, please do so." He has to command it because it is the Word of God.

The passage here says those who are married should not leave the spouse. It means they should not live separately or divorce. If they do, they should not remarry another person but remain single or be reconciled again with the spouse.

Unlike for unbelievers, it is not right for believers to separate or divorce. Even though there are differences in personalities and opinions, they should understand and yield to each other. It is the duty of believers to love, unite, and forgive.

It also says, "...the husband should not divorce his wife." It means the husband should not be the first to suggest divorce. Such words are only for unbelievers, not for believers.

Verse 12-13 says, "But to the rest I say, not the Lord, that if any brother has a wife who is an unbeliever, and she consents to live with him, he must not divorce her. And a woman who has an unbelieving husband, and he consents to live with her, she must not send her husband away." This is not the Word of God but Paul's opinion. But it is almost the same as God's will because the apostle Paul clearly heard the voice of the Holy Spirit and acted in the ways of the Lord.

The Law of the Old Testament told the Israelites not to marry Gentiles. Similarly, in the New Testament, the parallel is made that the believers should not marry unbelievers.

But then, how can there be a situation in which one of the couple is not a believer? Suppose two unbelievers marry and later one of them begins to attend church and becomes a believer. In this case, it is the best if the other spouse also follows the course in attending church and also accepting the Lord, but it may not be the case.

Consider the case of the wife not accepting the gospel. A believing husband cannot say, "I want a divorce because you are not attending church." If the unbelieving wife still wants to live with her believing husband, he should not divorce her.

Here, we see the situation that says, "if she consents to live with him." It's the same when the wife becomes a believer and the husband does not. But it doesn't mean one can divorce his/her spouse if the spouse does not consent to live with him/her.

For the unbelieving husband is sanctified through his wife, and the unbelieving wife is sanctified through her believing husband; for otherwise your children are unclean, but now they are holy. (7:14)

The passage said we shouldn't divorce an unbelieving husband or wife, and the reason is explained in this verse. For example, when the wife is a believer and her husband is not, the wife would pray for the salvation of her husband and try to evangelize him. Also, when the wife, who used to quarrel with her husband and get angry with him, becomes gentle and kindly serves the husband, he should eventually open his heart.

As the wife tells her husband her experiences in faith and delivers the Word of God, he may not seem to be interested at first, but it will be planted in his heart little by little. Finally, all these seeds will create a chance for him to accept the Lord. As the husband begins to attend church and live by the Word of the truth, he will gradually become sanctified.

It is much less common to have a believing husband and an unbelieving wife, but it's the same situation. If the husband leads the family as a good example, if he also helps with the house chores, and if, from time to time he gives his wife small gifts, shows attention to her and also loves her very much, the wife should also listen to him. Finally, she can also accept the gospel, listen to the Word, attend church, and finally become sanctified as well.

Verse 14 says, "...for otherwise your children are unclean, but now they are holy." What does it mean? In a case in which only one of the married couple attends church, the child is generally under more influence from the unbelieving parent.

Suppose the husband attends church and the wife does not. Then, the wife would not really listen to her husband. It usually means the wife is more stubborn than the husband. So, their children are influenced by the unbelieving mother and do not come to have faith.

Also, suppose the wife is a believer and the husband is not. In this case, the husband wouldn't listen to his wife but rather persecute her. Also, by his example he will teach his children not to attend church. Thus, verse 14 means that, when both the parents are not believers or when one of the parents is not a believer, it is not easy for their children to become sanctified.

At the end of the verse it says, "but now they are holy." Let me explain what it means. When one of the parents lives an exemplary life and constantly delivers the gospel to the other spouse, both of them will finally become believers. They will also change by the truth more and more. When the parents become holy, their children will also naturally become holy like their parents.

> **Yet if the unbelieving one leaves, let him leave; the brother or the sister is not under bondage in such *cases*, but God has called us to peace. For how do you know, O wife, whether you will save your husband? Or how do you know, O husband, whether you will save your wife? (7:15-16)**

This means, if the unbelieving husband or wife wants a divorce, the believing spouse can go ahead and get divorced. But it doesn't mean we should divorce an unbelieving spouse. This can be applied only in extreme situations.

For example, if the situation forces you to choose either your husband or the church, what would you do? You cannot choose your husband over choosing God and falling into Hell. If the husband also becomes violent and says, "I will divorce you before I let you attend church!" then it is not a sin to get divorced.

In this case, if she leaves God and turns her back on Him with the fear of being persecuted or getting divorced, it means she doesn't have faith in the first place. She chooses the way to Hell because she doesn't have faith.

Matthew 10:28 says, *"Do not fear those who kill the body but are unable to kill the soul; but rather fear Him who is able to destroy both soul and body in hell."* Men can kill the body, but not the soul.

Men may have control over physical life in this momentary world, but only God can put our soul either in Heaven or Hell. Therefore, we should fear God rather than man. We should obey the Word of God with reverent fear of Him.

But we should not lightly think we can divorce. We can understand the heart of God in the phrase, saying, "God has called us to peace." Namely, God wants us to have a peaceful and comfortable family. That is why we should try not to divorce, but to do everything we can to make our marriage lovely and pleasing, so that the unbelieving spouse can be saved through us.

According to the Measure of Faith

Only, as the Lord has assigned to each one, as God has called each, in this manner let him walk. And so I direct in all the churches. Was any man called *when he was already* circumcised? He is not to become uncircumcised. Has anyone been called in uncircumcision? He is not to be circumcised. (7:17-18)

The Lord gave us the gift of the Holy Spirit to lead us to the kingdom of Heaven. The Holy Spirit lets us realize the truth and recognize sin. The Holy Spirit saves us through our faith.

"Let him walk as God has called each," means we have to act according to the measure of our faith. We can just act according to the grace of the Lord which is given to the extent that our faith grows up.

We cannot put pressure on newcomers to the church by saying, "You have to close your shop on Sundays," or "You will be punished if you do not give tithes." To those babies who can only drink milk, if you give them solid food or meat, they will have a problem with it. We have to teach each one with wisdom according to the measure of each one's faith.

Then the passage says, "Was any man called *when he was already* circumcised? He is not to become uncircumcised. Has anyone been called in uncircumcision? He is not to be circumcised."

Men in Israel are circumcised on the 8th day of birth. It is the symbol of covenant that God made with Abraham saying, "I am your God who keeps you and leads you to salvation, and you are My people."

The physical purpose of circumcision is for reasons of cleanliness and sanitation. Spiritually it symbolizes establishing the covenant with God. In the Old Testament times, they did not receive the Holy Spirit. But through circumcision they could go before God. In the New Testament, we are not saved by our deeds, and so, we have to become circumcised in the heart to rid our hearts of unclean things by the Holy Spirit.

"To be called when one was already circumcised" means the person is one from among the people of God since he has the symbol of God's covenant. The uncircumcised refers to the Gentiles. Telling the circumcised not to become uncircumcised means they, as people of God, should live in the truth and not depart from faith. As God's children, we should not live just like the worldly people committing sins and compromising with the world, like the uncircumcised.

Also, "to be called when he was uncircumcised" means being called as a Gentile. So, telling a person not to get circumcised meant that the individual should not lead a Christian life like the Jews who practice the Law to receive salvation. Those who are called as a Gentile are saved through faith in Jesus Christ, not by the outward deeds.

The Difference between "Outward Deeds" and "Keeping the Commandments"

> Circumcision is nothing, and uncircumcision is nothing, but *what matters* is the keeping of the commandments of God. Each man must remain in that condition in which he was called. (7:19-20)

We came before God by His calling. So, we don't have to be circumcised like in the Old Testament. Such an act is not the way of salvation. Neither can it become our reward in Heaven.

Then, what do we have to do? The above passage tells us that we can show the evidence of our love for God and go the way of salvation by keeping of the commandments of God.

Some people may misunderstand what this means. Some people say, "Now we are living in New Testament, and we are not saved through the deeds of the Law. We are saved by faith." They say this because they do not understand what faith is.

Now, what is the difference between "outward deeds"

and "keeping of the commandments"? To keep God's commandments refers to the circumcision of heart. It is to cast away the unclean things not only in action but also from the heart and live a clean life according to the Word of God.

In the Old Testament, as long as they kept the Law outwardly, they didn't sin at all. For example, even if they had some adulterous thoughts when looking at a woman, it was not considered a sin for it was not something done, caused or committed in action.

But in the New Testament, to have such a mind is considered a sin. Furthermore, we have to cast away this unclean heart itself. Not only the deeds, but also when we cast away the untruthfulness of the heart from our inner being can we say we really keep the commandments.

It is useless just to follow the way of outward deeds without changing the heart, for we are not saved by our deeds. Even if we attend church on Sundays and give tithes, we cannot be saved if we do not live in the truth and still commit acts of unrighteousness. If we live in lawlessness without circumcising our heart, God cannot say we have faith.

That is why the apostle Paul tells us not to become the "circumcised" or the "uncircumcised," but only keep the commandments of God.

Romans 10:10 says, *"...for with the heart a person believes, resulting in righteousness, and with the mouth he confesses, resulting in salvation."* As recorded, those who believe in the heart will keep the commands of God. They will cast away sins from heart and keep what He commands. This way, they naturally circumcise their heart and become righteous.

Each man must remain in that condition in which he was called

Verse 20 says, "Each man must remain in that condition in which he was called." It means, once we accept Jesus Christ, we have to show our deeds and love in truth (1 John 3:18).

Some people say, "I cannot attend church because I am a drinker." Others may say they cannot attend church on Sunday because they "have to open their shops" or they offer other reasons for working on Sundays. But God says we should come before Him in our given situation and try our best to be faithful in deeds and truth.

> Were you called while a slave? Do not worry about it; but if you are able also to become free, rather do that. For he who was called in the Lord while a slave, is the Lord's freedman; likewise he who was called while free, is Christ's slave. (7:21-22)

Most people belong to some kind of organization or group. This passage tells us not to worry if we are called while we are bound by something else. Even though our body is bound by somebody or something, our heart can still seek God and follow the truth.

Of course, it would be much better to have freedom in our religion. It is better to work faithfully for the kingdom of God rather than to be bound. Therefore, both situations are OK, but of course, it is better to have freedom.

Verse 22 says, "For he who was called in the Lord while a slave, is the Lord's freedman;"

We belong to the Lord if we open our heart and accept Jesus Christ. In the passage, 'a slave' can be divided into two categories.

The first is a slave bound in the world. This does not mean just any slave in this world. But it refers to people who are slaves to a job in the world but offer their hearts to the Lord. When they keep the commands of the Lord with this kind of a heart, they will be freemen in the Lord as recorded in John 8:32 saying, *"and you will know the truth, and the truth will make you free."*

Also, there are slaves who are bound in the Lord. They are the servants and workers of God who work in the church serving God. They are also freemen in the Lord.

Some of the new believers, those who do not know the truth well, or those who were somewhat forced to take a duty in the church say that they are bound by the Lord and they have no freedom. They think they are bound by God or the church, but in fact, they are not bound but free. Why is it so?

If they are not called as servants of the Lord, whose servants would they have become? They must have become the servants of this world, the servants of the enemy devil and Satan. They were set free from these chains, and gained true freedom. And they are going the way of eternal life. This is in fact the true freedom.

If you become a pastor or take some duties in the church, it means you are working for the kingdom and righteousness of God, and for the brothers in faith. This is the way to receive eternal life, blessings on earth, and the rewards in Heaven.

It is the way for you to be spiritually and physically healthy, for your soul to prosper, and for your brothers in faith to be well off. This is the way of joy and the good way. So, we should do our best for the works of the Lord and gain true faith, peace, and freedom.

With regards to this, Paul said "he who was called while free," and right after that, why did he say such a person "is Christ's slave"? A slave has to unconditionally obey his master. A servant of God serves God as His master, and thus, he shouldn't have any of his own ideas but only follow God's idea, which is the truth.

Therefore, we are free to follow the way of eternal life. We are slaves who are bound within the truth before God. We can be truly free men when we become slaves in truth.

You were bought with a price; do not become slaves of men. Brethren, each one is to remain with God in

that *condition* in which he was called. (7:23-24)

To give us true life, God bought us with the precious blood of His one and only Son Jesus. Therefore, we are not ours, but God's. When we do not receive blessings it is because we do not give our lives to God. We can have true happiness and true freedom and we can also walk with God in prosperity when we give Him all we have.

As the apostle Paul confessed in 1 Corinthians 15:31 saying, *"I die daily,"* we should also die everyday and make ourselves obedient to the truth. Then, God can control our thoughts and minds. We will be able to hear the voice of the Holy Spirit clearly and be guided to the way of prosperity.

"Do not become slaves of men" does not mean that we should not be bound in a job of this world. It means that we should not follow the law of men that is against the truth. Jesus also said in Matthew 10:28, *"Do not fear those who kill the body but are unable to kill the soul; but rather fear Him who is able to destroy both soul and body in hell."*

Our body is only temporal and everyone dies, but our spirits last forever. Thus, we should not fear men who can kill the body but only God who manages our spirits.

At the time of Daniel, his king was deceived by the scheme of his ministers and issued a decree of prohibiting anyone from praying to any other god or man than the king himself for one month. But Daniel did not keep it because it was not in accordance with the truth.

Knowing he would be thrown into lion's den, he violated the law of the country to please God. He was not afraid of people who could kill his body, but feared only his God. He followed the law of God and finally God worked for the good of everything.

In Acts chapter 4, we see a scene in which the priests, rulers, elders, and scribes threatened the apostles ordering them not to preach about Jesus Christ. But Peter and John answered and said to them, *"Whether it is right in the sight of God to give heed to you rather than to God, you be the judge; for we cannot stop speaking about what we have seen and heard"* (v.19-20).

They meant they would follow the Word of God, not the words of men, because God commanded them to preach the gospel and not fear any persecutions. We should not become servants of men, but only obey the Word of God who bought us with the price and leads us to eternal life.

Verse 24 says, "Brethren, each one is to remain with God in that *condition* in which he was called." What does this mean? This means we can live in the condition in which we were called. We should not say, "I want to be faithful to God, and I will quit my job and only do God's ministry."

We have to live in the Word of God more and more, give out the fragrance of Christ, and give glory to God by saving other souls that are in the situation that we once found ourselves.

It Is Good for a Man to Remain as He Is

> Now concerning virgins I have no command of the Lord, but I give an opinion as one who by the mercy of the Lord is trustworthy. I think then that this is good in view of the present distress, that it is good for a man to remain as he is. (7:25-26)

Paul says he has no command concerning virgins. In the Bible, whether in Old Testament or New Testament, there is no guidance about the marriage of virgins. Our Lord is merciful, righteous, and full of love. Without any complaint, regret, or resentment, even under persecutions, the apostle Paul was faithful to the point of death for this Lord.

And this Paul gave his opinion. Since there was no specific command of God concerning virgins, he said in the next verse, "I give an opinion." But he was speaking according to the inspiration of the Holy Spirit. That is why he also emphasized the point saying, "as one who by the mercy of the Lord is trustworthy."

Verse 26 says in view of the present distress, it is good for a man to remain as he is. Believers know that their names are written in the book of life in Heaven. They also know that, when the Lord comes again, there will be the Great Tribulation, the Millennium Kingdom, and the Great White Throne Judgment. Here, by saying 'present distress', Paul did not mean that the Lord would come back in the air soon.

This is the distress that exists for everyone. Some die at a young age. Others, even with good health they live only for seventy or eighty years. Once they face physical death, they have no other choice but to stand before the judgment of God. Therefore, the distress is present for everybody, both for those who lived two thousand years ago and those who live today.

Paul said that it was good for a man to remain as he was. The next verse explains the reason why.

Are you bound to a wife? Do not seek to be released. Are you released from a wife? Do not seek a wife. But if you marry, you have not sinned; and if a virgin marries, she has not sinned. Yet such will have trouble in this life, and I am trying to spare you. (7:27-28)

Being bound to a wife means that the person is married. Verse 4 of this chapter says that the wife does not have authority over her own body, but the husband does. And likewise, the husband does not have authority over his own body, but the wife does. Husbands and wives are bound to each other, not having authority over their own bodies.

To be released is to separate or divorce, and so, "Do not seek to be released" means we should not seek divorce. Also, if we are already divorced or if our spouse died, Paul urges us to remain "as we are."

Of course, it is not sin to get married. The reason why Paul said this is because he loved them very much. Namely, we will have tribulations when we get married.

For example, if a man remains single, he can love God and be faithful to God as much as he wants. He can also take care of other souls and even offer all-night prayers, for he is not bound to anyone.

But if he is married, he will have some distress in life for he does not have as much freedom over his own life. He has to take the responsibility of his family by working hard. Even though he wants to do something for God, he may sometimes have to stay with his wife and children. Especially, in case of women, they may not even be able to attend church on Sundays if the husband does not have any faith.

But this I say, brethren, the time has been shortened, so that from now on those who have wives should be as though they had none; and those who weep, as though they did not weep; and those who rejoice, as though

they did not rejoice; and those who buy, as though they did not possess; and those who use the world, as though they did not make full use of it; for the form of this world is passing away. (7:29-31)

This passage clearly illustrates to us what kind of life believers have to lead in a time where the Lord's Second Coming is near.

It says, "those who have wives should be as though they had none." It does not mean we should get divorced! However, though one is bound to his wife, there shouldn't be a case in which he does not do what he is supposed to do for God because he cares more dearly for his wife. He has to give what has to be given to God, yet he also has to be faithful to his family. He has to fulfill his duty as a husband. But he shouldn't put his wife before God.

It also says, "...those who weep, as though they did not weep." Though there are many tears, sorrow, and pains in this world, we should rejoice and give thanks in the hope of the kingdom of Heaven even in tests and trials. We have to live in the grace of God preparing our oil in our lamp.

Then, what does it mean by "and those who rejoice, as though they did not rejoice"?

Suppose you received blessings and you are happy. But, if you go to a person who is grieving and show your happiness saying that you have received blessings, then that person may grieve even more. Therefore, we have to be prudent in considering the situation.

Then it says, "…those who buy, as though they did not possess." It means those who are rich on earth should not try to show that they are rich. Even if we are very wealthy, it will become nothing when the Lord comes back. We should not boast of the things that perish and disappear; we are to be content with the things we have and be faithful to God.

As we near the Second Coming of the Lord, those who use the things in the world have to be as those who do not make use of them. Many things of this world are used for idolatry, extravagance, pleasure, and gambling, and these are not righteous in the sight of God.

Therefore, we should have self-control over those things. We should not live in such luxury that causes brothers in faith to stumble. Furthermore, if a person indulges in luxury when the situation for it is not proper, people will regard them to be worthless.

The reason why we have to do all the above things is because everything in the world will pass away. Everything on earth is meaningless, and it will eventually perish. We cannot take anything physical with us from this earth when the Lord calls us. Everything will return to nothing. If the wealth and abundance that we enjoy makes others stumble, it is right not to keep those things.

But I want you to be free from concern. One who is unmarried is concerned about the things of the Lord,

how he may please the Lord; but one who is married is concerned about the things of the world, how he may please his wife, and *his interests* are divided. The woman who is unmarried, and the virgin, is concerned about the things of the Lord, that she may be holy both in body and spirit; but one who is married is concerned about the things of the world, how she may please her husband. (7:32-34)

The Lord said in Luke 16:13, *"You cannot serve God and wealth."* This is telling us that we must not be double-minded. A man who is not married is able to seek only God. He will spend his leisure time in pleasing God and working for God's kingdom and righteousness.

But when he gets married, he has to care for his family and other things of the world, so it is more difficult for him to be faithful to God.

In case of women, widows or single women, they too would be able to concentrate on pleasing God in their lives. They can strive to live a holy life trying to adorn themselves as brides of the Lord.

But when they are married, their mind is divided. They must think about such things as how they can please their husband, maintain their appearance, and receive his love and attention. Of course, it does not mean these things are bad. A wife should do so. If she can it is better for her to receive love from her husband and make a happy family.

This I say for your own benefit; not to put a restraint upon you, but to promote what is appropriate and *to secure* undistracted devotion to the Lord. (7:35)

Paul talked about the drawbacks of getting married, and now in this verse, he says it is better to offer ourselves to the Lord without any blemish or spot having the hope for and knowing about the rewards in the kingdom of Heaven.

Paul said those things not to cause us burden, but to be for our personal benefits. He explains what is more beneficial and why. Getting married is not a sin, and if you desire to marry, you should not let the above verses bind you to something you do not earnestly desire.

Furthermore, it certainly is not an ordinary kind of faith if you can offer yourself as a single man/woman in these days. You can do it only when you love God to the utmost degree, and therefore, you shouldn't carelessly make a vow that you will not get married.

Of course, if you truly realize the love of God deep in your heart and if you are so thankful for it, God will joyfully accept when you only live for Him alone. If you serve God and also serve this world, you will be busy and distracted. That is why Paul explained logically in delivering the will of God to us.

The Circumstances of Parents of a Virgin Daughter or for Widows and Widowers

But if any man thinks that he is acting unbecomingly toward his virgin *daughter*, if she is past her youth, and if it must be so, let him do what he wishes, he does not sin; let her marry. But he who stands firm in his heart, being under no constraint, but has authority over his own will, and has decided this in his own heart, to keep his own virgin *daughter*, he will do well. So then both he who gives his own virgin *daughter* in marriage does well, and he who does not give her in marriage will do better. (7:36-38)

Paul is speaking to a father who has a daughter who is old enough to get married. The father has a considerable measure of faith and he doesn't want his daughter to get married. But Paul also explains the case in which there is opposition against this father's idea by saying, "...that he is acting unbecomingly towards his virgin daughter."

For example, the mother of the daughter insists that their daughter get married or the daughter herself wants to get married. So, in the faith of the father, he doesn't want his daughter to get married. But when there are other situations, persecutions, or tests on the father because of his daughter not getting married, then, it is OK to let her be married, for it is not a sin to get married.

The opposite case is explained in verse 37. The father who has a virgin daughter has firm faith and he wants to suggest that his daughter walk the way of blessing. There is no other situation, any persecution, or test. In this kind of case, being under no constraint, if he has authority over his own will and has decided to keep his own virgin daughter, he will do well.

Today, parents may not have such authority, but long ago, people got married according to the will of their parents. But today, the opinion of the children counts more than that of the parents.

It is better in faith to keep a virgin daughter, but you don't have to worry about it. It is just better in God's sight that a single woman remains single. It is not a sin or transgression to get married.

A wife is bound as long as her husband lives; but if her husband is dead, she is free to be married to whom she wishes, only in the Lord. But in my opinion she is happier if she remains as she is; and I think that I also

have the Spirit of God. (7:39-40)

When a woman gets married, as in 1 Corinthians 7:4, she is bound to her husband. But if the husband is dead, she has freedom to get married again. But that has to happen only in the Lord, which means she has to find a husband among the believers. A believer ought to find his/her spouse among the believers. Much is said about this in both the Old and New Testament.

Some say, "Isn't it good for a believer to meet an unbeliever and guide that person to God?" If that can happen, then it would be very good. But in most cases, that doesn't happen.

Once, a female church member consulted me. She had been attending church before she got married, and when her husband proposed to her, he was not a believer. So she refused him saying she couldn't marry an unbeliever. Then, that man also began to attend church and finally, they got married.

But he changed his mind after the marriage and stopped attending church. Furthermore, not only that he didn't attend church, but he persecuted his wife for attending church, too. It was a very pitiful case.

The enemy devil and Satan incite some people around us to take away our faith. Like a roaring lion the devil looks for someone to devour. Unless we stand on the rock of faith, we can be deceived by Satan and in compromise, and we may even depart from God.

Verse 40 explains which option is better. We have the

freedom of choice whether or not to get married, but it is proper to do it in the Lord. But the verse says it is better for those who have love and passion for God to remain single.

Also, the reason why Paul said, "and I think that I also have the Spirit of God," is because people might have thought it was merely Paul's personal opinion, for he had said, 'in my opinion'.

This verse has two meanings to consider. One is: "I have received the Holy Spirit, and I am speaking according to the Holy Spirit." The other is: "I am also dedicated to God without getting married. I have chosen what is better in accordance with the will of the Holy Spirit."

The Author
Dr. Jaerock Lee

Dr. Jaerock Lee was born in Muan, Jeonnam Province, Republic of Korea, in 1943. In his twenties, he suffered from a variety of incurable diseases for seven years and awaited death with no hope for recovery. One day in the spring of 1974, however, he was led to a church by his sister, and when he knelt down to pray, the living God immediately healed him of all his diseases.

From the moment Dr. Lee met the living God through that wonderful experience, he has loved God with all his heart and sincerity, and in 1978 was called to be a servant of God. He prayed fervently so that he could clearly understand the will of God and wholly accomplish it, and obeyed all the Word of God. In 1982, he founded Manmin Church in Seoul, S. Korea, and countless works of God, including miraculous healings and wonders, have been taking place at his church.

In 1986, Dr. Lee was ordained as a pastor at the Annual Assembly of Jesus' Sungkyul Church of Korea, and four years later in 1990, his sermons began to be broadcast on the Far East Broadcasting Company, the Asia Broadcast Station, and the Washington Christian Radio System to Australia, Russia, the Philippines, and many more.

Three years later in 1993, Manmin Central Church was selected as one of the "World's Top 50 Churches" by the *Christian World* magazine (US) and he received an Honorary Doctorate of Divinity from Christian Faith College, Florida, USA, and in 1996 a Ph. D. in Ministry from Kingsway Theological Seminary, Iowa, USA.

Since 1993, Dr. Lee has taken the lead in world mission through many overseas crusades in Israel, L.A., New York City, Baltimore City, Hawaii of the USA, Tanzania, Argentina, Uganda, Japan, Pakistan, Kenya, the Philippines, Honduras, India, Russia, Germany, Peru, and Democratic Republic of Congo, and in 2002 he was called a "worldwide pastor" by major Christian newspapers in Korea for his work in various overseas crusades.

As of March 2010, Manmin Central Church is a congregation of more than 100,000 members and has 9,000 branch churches throughout the globe including 52 domestic branch churches in major cities, and has so far commissioned more than 131 missionaries to 23 countries, including the United States, Russia, Germany, Canada, Japan, China, France, India, Kenya, and many more.

To this day, Dr. Lee has written 59 books, including bestsellers *Tasting Eternal Life before Death*, *My Life My Faith I & II*, *The Message of the Cross*, *The Measure of Faith*, *Heaven I & II*, and *Hell*, and his works have been being translated into more than 44 languages.

His Christian columns appear on *The Hankook Ilbo*, *The JoongAng Daily*, *The Dong-A Ilbo*, *The Munhwa Ilbo*, *The Seoul Shinmun*, *The Kyunghyang Shinmun*, *The Hankyoreh Shinmun*, *The Korea Economic Daily*, *The Korea Herald*, *The Shisa News*, and *The Christian Press*.

Dr. Lee is currently leader of many missionary organizations and associations including: Chairman, The United Holiness Church of Jesus Christ; Permanent President of the World Christianity Revival Mission Association; President, Manmin World Mission; Founder, Manmin TV; Founder & Board Chairman, Global Christian Network (GCN); Founder & Board Chairman, World Christian Doctors Network (WCDN); and Founder & Board Chairman, Manmin International Seminary (MIS).

Heaven I & II

A detailed sketch of the gorgeous living environment the heavenly citizens enjoy and beautiful description of different levels of heavenly kingdoms.

The Message of the Cross

A powerful awakening message for all the people who are spiritually asleep In this book you will find the reason Jesus is the only Savior and the true love of God.

Hell

An earnest message to all mankind from God, who wishes not even one soul to fall into the depths of hell! You will discover the never-before-revealed account of the cruel reality of the Lower Grave and hell.

Tasting Eternal Life Before Death

A testimonial memoirs of Dr. Jaerock Lee, who was born gain and saved from the valley of death and has been leading an exemplary Christian life.

The Measure of Faith

What kind of a dwelling place, crown and reward are prepared for you in heaven? This book provides with wisdom and guidance for you to measure your faith and cultivate the best and most mature faith.

www.ingramcontent.com/pod-product-compliance
Lightning Source LLC
Chambersburg PA
CBHW061606120626
46550CB00004B/1623